Behavior Mastery

Jack Hill

Published by Jack Hill, 2024.

BEHAVIOR MASTERY

First edition. August 2, 2024.

Copyright © 2024 Jack Hill.

ISBN: 979-8227201423

Written by Jack Hill.

Table of Contents

Behavior Mastery

The Power of Small Actions

By

Jack Hill

Copyright©2024 Jack Hill

The Story behind - Behavior Mastery: The Power of Small Actions

In the bustling heart of New York City, where the pace of life is relentless and dreams are as vast as the skyline, my journey of writing *Behavior Mastery: The Power of Small Actions* began. It wasn't a grand revelation or a sudden stroke of genius, but rather the quiet moments of everyday life where small actions began to shape a new reality.

A few years ago, I found myself in a rut. Professionally, I was doing well, but personally, I felt stuck. My days were a blur of meetings, emails, and endless to-do lists. I was living in a cycle of productivity without purpose, overwhelmed by the constant pressure to achieve more. It was during a rare moment of reflection, late one night, that I realized I needed a change.

I remembered a concept I had come across in my readings: the power of small actions. The idea that tiny, consistent steps could lead to significant transformation intrigued me. But it wasn't until I decided to put this theory into practice that its true power became evident.

I started with the simplest of actions. Every morning, before diving into the chaos of my day, I spent five minutes in quiet reflection. I focused on my breathing, set a positive intention for the day, and expressed gratitude for the little things. This seemingly insignificant habit began to create a ripple effect. I found myself approaching my tasks with more clarity and less stress.

Encouraged by this small success, I began to incorporate other tiny habits into my routine. I set a goal to read one page of a book every day. Just one page. This small commitment soon turned into a chapter, and before I knew it, I was finishing books that had long been gathering dust on my shelf. These books, filled with insights on psychology, neuroscience, and human behavior, deepened my understanding of how habits shape our lives.

As I delved deeper into the science of habits, I realized the profound impact these small actions were having on my life. I felt in control, close to my goals, and purposeful. It was during a quiet evening, while reflecting on my journey, that the idea for *Behavior Mastery: The Power of Small Actions* was born.

I wanted to share this transformative power with others. I wanted to show that anyone, regardless of their circumstances, could create meaningful change through small, deliberate actions. But I knew that for the book to resonate, it needed to be rooted in real, lived experiences. As a result, I decided to weave my own story into its pages.

Writing this book was not without its challenges. On certain days, doubt crept in, and the enormity of the task felt overwhelming. But I applied the very principles I was writing about. I broke the writing process down into small, manageable steps. I committed to writing just one paragraph each day. Some days, that paragraph turned into pages. On other days, it remained a single paragraph. But the key was consistency.

I also reached out to others who had embraced the power of small actions. I interviewed athletes, artists, entrepreneurs, and everyday individuals who had transformed their lives through tiny habits. Their stories added depth and richness to the book, reinforcing the universal applicability of these principles.

Throughout this journey, one of the most powerful lessons I learned was the importance of reflection. Taking time to pause and reflect on my progress, to celebrate small wins, and to learn from setbacks became an integral part of my process. This practice not only kept me motivated but also provided valuable insights that enriched the content of the book.

As I neared completion of Behavior Mastery: The Power of Small Actions, I began to see the ripple effect of my work. Friends and colleagues who had witnessed my transformation began to take small actions in their own lives. They reported feeling more focused, more energized, and more fulfilled. It was incredibly rewarding to see the principles I was writing about making a tangible difference in the lives of others.

Today, as I hold the finished book in my hands, I am filled with a sense of accomplishment and gratitude. This book is not just a collection of theories and strategies; it is a testament to the power of small actions. It is a reminder that meaningful change is within everyone's reach, no matter how daunting the journey may seem.

My invitation to you is "Behavior Mastery: The Power of Small Actions." It is a call to embrace the small steps that lead to big transformations. It is a guide to help you navigate the path of habit formation, arming you with the knowledge that every small action you take brings you closer to the person you aspire to be.

So, start today. Take that first small step. Reflect on your progress. Celebrate your wins. And remember, the journey to behavior mastery begins with the power of small actions.

Introduction

In a world that often celebrates grand gestures and monumental achievements, it's easy to overlook the subtle yet profound power of small actions. "Behavior Mastery: The Power of Small Actions" invites readers to shift their focus from the towering peaks of success to the incremental steps that pave the way. This book is not about overnight transformations or drastic changes; it's about the quiet revolution that takes place within us when we harness the power of tiny, consistent behaviors.

The journey to behavior mastery begins with understanding the science behind habits. Habits are the brain's way of automating repetitive actions to conserve mental energy. From brushing our teeth to our morning commute, these routines form the bedrock of our daily lives. Yet, while some habits propel us toward our goals, others can impede our progress. Recognizing and reshaping these habits is crucial for personal and professional growth.

James Clear, in his influential book "Atomic Habits," has already illustrated the significant impact of small habits. Building upon this foundation, "Behavior Mastery: The Power of Small Actions" delves deeper into the psychological and neurological mechanisms that underpin our daily behaviors. The design of this book equips readers with practical strategies rooted in scientific research, thereby enhancing the accessibility and effectiveness of habit formation.

The compound effect principle is at the heart of behavior mastery. Just as compound interest turns a small investment into a substantial fortune over time, small actions, when performed consistently, can lead to remarkable results. Consider the story of an Olympic athlete who trains rigorously every day, not just focusing on winning medals but perfecting each minor aspect of their routine. These small, incremental improvements accumulate, resulting in peak performance. The same principle applies to any area of life, whether it's personal development, career advancement, or health and fitness.

However, the path to mastering behaviors is not always straightforward. One of the major challenges is the gap between our intentions and our actions. We often set ambitious goals, driven by a burst of motivation, only to falter when faced with the realities of daily life. This discrepancy arises because goals set the direction, but systems drive progress. "Behavior Mastery: The Power of Small Actions" emphasizes the importance of developing effective systems that make desirable behaviors automatic and undesirable behaviors difficult.

A key component of these systems is the habit loop, which comprises three elements: cue, routine, and reward. Understanding how these components interact allows us to strategically design our environments to support positive habits. For example, if you want to read more, placing a book on your bedside table serves as a cue, establishing a routine of reading before bed, and creating a sense of relaxation and satisfaction as a reward. Over time, this loop reinforces the habit, making it an integral part of your daily life.

The book also explores the concept of keystone habits, which are foundational behaviors that trigger a cascade of positive changes in other areas. Identifying and cultivating these keystone habits can create a domino effect, leading to comprehensive behavior mastery. For example, regular exercise is a keystone habit that not only improves physical health but also enhances mental clarity, boosts mood, and fosters discipline.

But what happens when we encounter obstacles, such as a lack of motivation and willpower? "Behavior Mastery: The Power of Small Actions" addresses these challenges head-on. Motivation is often fleeting, and willpower can be easily depleted. Therefore, relying solely on these factors is a recipe for inconsistency. Instead, the book advocates for strategies that reduce friction and make beneficial habits easier to perform. This includes techniques like habit stacking, where you pair a new habit with an existing one, and environmental design, which involves modifying your surroundings to promote success.

Identity is a frequently overlooked aspect of habit formation. The beliefs we hold about ourselves significantly influence our actions. If you view yourself as someone who is health-conscious, you are more likely to adopt healthy habits. "Behavior Mastery: The Power of Small Actions" encourages readers to align their habits with their desired identity, creating a powerful feedback loop where actions reinforce beliefs, and beliefs drive actions.

Tracking progress and maintaining accountability are also critical components of behavior mastery. Keeping a habit journal or using apps can help monitor your progress, providing tangible evidence of improvement and areas that need adjustment. Additionally, involving others in your journey, whether through accountability partners or support groups, can provide the encouragement and reinforcement needed to stay on track.

The book is rich with real-life examples and stories from diverse fields, illustrating how small actions have led to extraordinary achievements. From the meticulous routines of artists and athletes to the daily practices of business leaders and healthcare professionals, these stories serve as both inspiration and proof of the power of small actions.

"Behavior Mastery: The Power of Small Actions" is more than just a guide to forming habits; it's a manifesto for a new way of living. It challenges the notion that change must be radical to be effective, offering instead a blueprint for gradual, sustainable transformation. By focusing on the minutiae of daily behaviors, this book provides the tools to build a foundation for lasting success.

As you embark on this journey through the pages of "Behavior Mastery: The Power of Small Actions," you will discover that the key to unlocking your potential lies not in the grand gestures but in the small, consistent actions that shape your everyday life. With the power of small actions, you can achieve behavior mastery and transform your life in profound and lasting ways.

Chapter One

The Science of Small Actions

In the vast landscape of personal development, the notion of small actions stands as a formidable force, often underestimated but profoundly impactful. This chapter delves into the psychological and neurological foundations of habit formation, elucidates why small actions are remarkably effective in creating lasting change, and examines the compound effect of these tiny behaviors over time.

The Psychological and Neurological Foundations of Habit Formation

At the heart of habit formation lies the brain's innate drive for efficiency. Habits are mental shortcuts that the brain forms to save energy and streamline decision-making processes. This phenomenon is rooted in the basal ganglia, a part of the brain responsible for motor control and procedural learning. When a behavior is repeated consistently, it becomes encoded in the basal ganglia, allowing it to be performed with minimal conscious effort.

The process of habit formation can be broken down into three distinct stages: cue, routine, and reward, often referred to as the habit loop. A cue is a trigger that initiates the behavior; a routine is the behavior itself; and a reward is the positive reinforcement that follows, solidifying the habit. Over time, this loop becomes increasingly automatic as the brain begins to associate the cue with the reward, bypassing the need for deliberate thought.

The prefrontal cortex, the part of the brain responsible for decision-making and self-control, also plays a crucial role in habit formation. However, the prefrontal cortex is resource-intensive and can easily become fatigued. This is where small actions come into play. By breaking down behaviors into manageable, bite-sized tasks, we can reduce the cognitive load on the prefrontal cortex, making it easier to form and maintain new habits.

The Effectiveness of Small Actions in Creating Lasting Change

SMALL ACTIONS ARE UNIQUELY effective in creating lasting change for several reasons. First, they lower the barrier to entry. When a task is perceived as overwhelming, it triggers the brain's aversion response, leading to procrastination and avoidance. On the other hand, small actions are less intimidating and more achievable, reducing resistance and increasing the likelihood of initiation.

Moreover, small actions build momentum. The psychological principle of consistency, as described by Dr. Robert Cialdini in his book "Influence," suggests that once we commit to a small action, we are more likely to follow through with subsequent actions that align with our initial commitment. This creates a positive feedback loop, where each small success reinforces our motivation and confidence, propelling us forward.

Another critical aspect is the role of intrinsic motivation. Small actions often align better with our intrinsic motivation, the internal desire to perform a behavior for its own sake rather than for an external reward. When we start small, we can focus on the process rather than the outcome, fostering a sense of enjoyment and satisfaction that sustains our efforts over the long term.

Furthermore, small actions are easier to integrate into our existing routines. The concept of habit stacking, popularized by James Clear, involves pairing a new habit with an existing one, creating a seamless transition. For instance, if you want to develop the habit of reading more, you could start by reading for just five minutes during your morning coffee routine. Over time, this small action can grow into a substantial and ingrained habit.

The Compound Effect of Tiny Behaviors Over Time

THE COMPOUND EFFECT, a concept famously articulated by Darren Hardy, posits that small, consistent actions, when compounded over time, yield significant results. This principle can be likened to the mathematical concept of exponential growth, where each increment builds upon the previous one, leading to a rapid escalation in the overall impact.

Consider the example of physical fitness. If you commit to doing just ten push-ups every day, it may seem inconsequential initially. However, over the course of a year, this small action accumulates to 3,650 push-ups, resulting in noticeable strength gains and improved fitness. The same principle applies to other areas of life, such as learning, financial management, and personal development.

For example, dedicating just 15 minutes a day to reading can lead to the completion of numerous books over the course of a year, significantly expanding your knowledge and perspective in the realm of learning. Financially, saving a small amount of money regularly can compound into a substantial nest egg over time, thanks to the power of compound interest.

The compound effect also operates on a psychological level. Each small action we take sends a signal to our brain, reinforcing our identity and shaping our self-image. When we consistently engage in behaviors that align with our goals, we begin to see ourselves as the type of person who embodies those qualities. This shift in self-perception fuels further positive behaviors, creating a virtuous cycle of growth and improvement.

Small actions have a ripple effect.

Beyond individual benefits, small actions can create a ripple effect, influencing others and fostering a culture of positive change. New habits often inspire others to adopt them. This social contagion effect can amplify the impact of our small actions, leading to collective improvements within families, communities, and organizations.

For instance, a leader who prioritizes small actions for personal growth can set a powerful example for their team, fostering an environment where continuous improvement is valued and practiced. Similarly, parents who model healthy habits can instill those behaviors in their children, promoting their lifelong well-being.

"Behavior Mastery: The Power of Small Actions" underscores the profound impact of tiny behaviors on personal and collective transformation. By understanding the psychological and neurological foundations of habit formation, recognizing the effectiveness of small actions, and appreciating the compound effect over time, we can harness this power to create lasting, meaningful change. In a world that often overlooks the small in favor of the grand, this book serves as a reminder that true mastery lies in the consistent, incremental steps we take every day. The science of small actions reveals the potential to reshape our lives and the world around us.

Chapter Two

Identifying Your Keystone Habits

Habits form the foundation of our daily lives, dictating our actions and ultimately shaping our future. Among these myriad habits, there exists a special category known as keystone habits—those fundamental routines that trigger a cascade of positive changes across various aspects of our lives. Understanding and identifying keystone habits is crucial for anyone seeking to achieve lasting personal transformation. This chapter delves into the definition and importance of keystone habits, provides a guide for identifying your own, and shares examples of influential keystone habits from different fields.

Defining Keystone Habits and Their Importance

Keystone habits are pivotal behaviors that have a disproportionate impact on our lives. Unlike regular habits, which may affect a specific area, keystone habits create a ripple effect, influencing other behaviors and routines. They act as catalysts for broader change, setting off a chain reaction that improves multiple aspects of our lives.

The importance of keystone habits lies in their ability to streamline our efforts toward personal growth. By focusing on a few key behaviors, we can indirectly influence a wide range of outcomes. For example, consider the habit of regular exercise. This keystone habit not only improves physical health but also enhances mental well-being, boosts energy levels, fosters discipline, and even encourages healthier eating habits. The interconnected nature of keystone habits makes them incredibly powerful tools for achieving holistic improvement.

Identifying Your Own Keystone Habits

FINDING YOUR KEYSTONE habits requires introspection and a strategic approach. Here are steps to help you identify these transformative behaviors:

Assess Your Goals and Values: Start by reflecting on your long-term goals and core values. What do you want to achieve, and what matters most to you? Understanding your priorities will guide you in identifying habits that align with your aspirations.

Analyze Your Current Habits: Take an inventory of your existing habits. Which ones contribute positively to your life, and which ones hinder your progress? Look for patterns and connections between different behaviors.

Identify Key Areas of Impact: Consider the areas of your life that you want to improve, such as health, productivity, relationships, or personal development. Keystone habits often address multiple areas simultaneously.

Seek Patterns of Influence: Observe how certain habits influence other behaviors. A keystone habit will typically have a cascading effect, leading to positive changes in various domains. For instance, a morning routine that includes meditation might not only reduce stress but also enhance focus and productivity throughout the day.

Experiment and Reflect: Try adopting potential keystone habits and observe their impact over time. Keep a journal to document the changes you experience. Reflect on how these habits affect your overall well-being and progress toward your goals.

Consult with Others: Sometimes, an outside perspective can provide valuable insights. Discuss your habits with friends, family, or mentors who know you well. They might help you identify patterns you hadn't noticed.

Examples of Influential Keystone Habits from Various Fields

TO ILLUSTRATE THE POWER of keystone habits, let's explore some examples from different fields:

Health and Fitness: Regular Exercise

Regular exercise is a quintessential keystone habit. Beyond its direct benefits of improved physical fitness and health, exercise influences numerous other aspects of life. It improves mental clarity, boosts mood through endorphin release, and promotes better sleep. Additionally, the discipline and routine established through regular exercise often spill over into other areas, such as healthier eating and increased productivity.

Personal Development: Morning Routines

ESTABLISHING A STRUCTURED morning routine can set a positive tone for the entire day. A morning routine might include activities like meditation, journaling, exercise, and goal-setting. This keystone habit helps cultivate a mindset of intention and preparedness, leading to improved time management, reduced stress, and greater overall productivity.

Professional Success: Time Management

EFFECTIVE TIME MANAGEMENT is a keystone habit that significantly impacts professional success. By prioritizing tasks, setting goals, and maintaining a schedule, individuals can enhance their productivity and efficiency. Good time management also reduces stress and allows for better work-life balance, which in turn positively affects personal relationships and well-being.

Relationships: Active Listening

ACTIVE LISTENING IS a powerful keystone habit for building and maintaining strong relationships. When individuals make a habit of genuinely listening to others, it fosters deeper connections, enhances empathy, and reduces misunderstandings. This habit can improve both personal and professional relationships, leading to greater satisfaction and cooperation.

Financial stability: Regular savings

CULTIVATING THE HABIT of regular savings is essential for financial stability and long-term security. This keystone habit encourages disciplined spending, reduces financial stress, and provides a safety net for emergencies. Over time, regular savings can lead to significant financial growth and investment opportunities.

Learning and Growth: Daily Reading

INCORPORATING DAILY reading into your routine is a keystone habit that promotes continuous learning and intellectual growth. Whether it's reading books, articles, or research papers, this habit broadens your knowledge base, enhances critical thinking skills, and stimulates creativity. The insights gained from regular reading can be applied across various areas of life, from personal development to professional expertise.

The ripple Effect of Keystone Habits

THE TRUE POWER OF KEYSTONE habits lies in their ability to create a ripple effect. When you adopt a keystone habit, you often develop other positive habits. For instance, starting a regular exercise routine might inspire you to improve your diet, which in turn enhances your energy levels and productivity. This interconnectedness amplifies the impact of keystone habits, making them invaluable tools for comprehensive personal transformation.

Additionally, keystone habits can inspire those around you. When others observe the positive changes in your life, they may be motivated to adopt similar habits. This social contagion effect can lead to a broader culture of improvement within families, communities, and organizations.

Identifying and cultivating keystone habits is a strategic approach to achieving lasting personal transformation. By understanding the defining characteristics and importance of these habits and by carefully assessing and experimenting with potential keystone habits, individuals can unlock a cascade of positive changes across multiple domains. The examples from various fields highlight the profound impact that keystone habits can have, not only on individual lives but also on the broader social environment. Embrace the power of keystone habits and set yourself on a path of continuous growth and improvement. Through the transformative potential of these fundamental behaviors, you can achieve holistic success and fulfillment.

Chapter Three

The Habit Loop: Cue, Routine, and Reward

Habits are the building blocks of our daily lives, often operating beneath our conscious awareness. To harness their power and create positive change, it's essential to understand the mechanics behind them. This chapter explores the habit loop framework, which consists of three critical components: cue, routine, and reward. By breaking down how these elements interact to form habits and providing strategies for modifying each one, we can develop new, beneficial habits that stick.

Breaking down the Habit Loop Framework

The habit loop framework, popularized by Charles Duhigg in his book The Power of Habit, comprises three core components:

The cue is a trigger that initiates the habit. It can be anything that prompts the behavior, such as a specific time of day, an emotional state, a location, or the presence of certain people. Cues are the stimuli that signal the brain to enter automatic mode and execute the associated routine.

The routine is the behavior itself—the action that you take in response to the cue. This can be a physical activity, a mental process, or an emotional response. The routine is the most visible part of the habit, and we often focus on changing it.

Reward: The reward is the positive reinforcement you receive after completing the routine, you receive positive reinforcement. Rewards can be tangible, like a treat or a paycheck, or intangible, like a sense of accomplishment or a reduction in stress. The reward's role is to satisfy a craving and signal to the brain that the behavior is worth remembering and repeating.

Understanding these components is crucial because it allows us to dissect our habits and identify the triggers and rewards that sustain them. By analyzing the habit loop, we can pinpoint where to intervene and make changes.

How Cues, Routines, and Rewards Interact to Form Habits

HABITS ARE FORMED THROUGH a process of reinforcement, where the brain learns to associate specific cues with particular routines and rewards. Here's how the components interact:

Cue and Craving: The cue triggers a craving for the reward, creating a sense of anticipation. This craving drives us to perform the routine, seeking the pleasure or relief that the reward provides.

Routine and Behavior: When the craving is strong enough, we engage in a routine. This behavior is the response to the cue and is carried out in anticipation of the reward.

Reward and Reinforcement: After completing the routine, we receive the reward, which satisfies the craving. This reward reinforces the cue-routine association in the brain, making the behavior more likely to be repeated.

Over time, this loop becomes more ingrained, and the behavior becomes automatic. The brain learns to predict the reward whenever the cue appears, and the routine is executed with minimal conscious effort.

Strategies for Modifying Each Element to Develop New Habits

TO DEVELOP NEW HABITS, we can modify each element of the habit loop. Here are strategies for addressing cues, routines, and rewards:

Modifying the Cue

IDENTIFY EXISTING CUES: Start by identifying the cues that trigger your current habits. Keep a habit journal to track when and where the behavior occurs, including the time of day, location, emotional state, and people around you.

Choose a Consistent Cue: For new habits, select a consistent and specific cue that can easily fit into your daily routine. This could be a time-based cue, such as waking up or after lunch, or an environmental cue, like entering a particular room or sitting at your desk.

Pair with Existing Habits: Utilize the strategy of habit stacking, where you pair the new habit with an existing one. For instance, if you want to start meditating, you could do it right after brushing your teeth in the morning.

Altering the Routine

SIMPLIFY THE ROUTINE: Make the new routine as simple and easy as possible to reduce resistance. Start with small, manageable actions that can be gradually expanded over time.

Plan and Prepare: Remove obstacles that might prevent you from engaging in the new routine. If you want to exercise in the morning, lay out your workout clothes the night before. Preparation makes it easier to stick to the routine.

Use Implementation Intentions: Formulate specific plans using the format "When X happens, I will do Y." For example, "When I finish dinner, I will spend 10 minutes reading a book."

Enhancing the Reward

MAKE REWARDS IMMEDIATE: Ensure the reward is immediate and satisfying. The brain responds better to instant gratification, so find ways to make the reward quickly follow the routine. If the reward is too delayed, the association between the behavior and the reward weakens.

Celebrate Small Wins: Acknowledge and celebrate small achievements along the way. Positive reinforcement boosts motivation and reinforces the habit. This could be as simple as giving yourself a mental pat on the back or sharing your success with a friend.

Find Intrinsic Rewards: Align the routine with activities that provide intrinsic satisfaction. If the behavior itself is enjoyable or fulfilling, the need for external rewards diminishes. For instance, if you enjoy the feeling of relaxation after meditating, the practice becomes self-reinforcing.

Examples of Applying the Habit Loop Framework

TO ILLUSTRATE THE APPLICATION of the habit loop framework, consider the goal of developing a habit of regular exercise:

Cue: Choose a consistent cue, such as setting an alarm for the same time each morning or placing your workout clothes next to your bed.

Routine: Start with a simple routine, like a 5-minute walk or a quick stretch. As this becomes a habit, gradually increase the duration and intensity of your workouts.

Reward: Provide an immediate reward, such as listening to your favorite podcast during the workout or enjoying a nutritious smoothie afterward.

Additionally, recognize the intrinsic rewards, such as increased energy and improved mood.

By consistently applying this framework, the exercise habit becomes ingrained, leading to lasting health benefits.

The habit loop framework—comprising cue, routine, and reward—is a powerful tool for understanding and shaping our behaviors. By breaking down this loop, we gain insights into the mechanics of habit formation and learn how to intervene effectively. Through strategic modifications to cues, routines, and rewards, we can cultivate new habits that align with our goals and values. Whether it's exercising regularly, improving productivity, or fostering better relationships, mastering the habit loop empowers us to make lasting, positive changes in our lives.

Chapter Four

Designing Your Environment for Success

Our environment profoundly impacts our behavior, shaping our habits in ways we often underestimate. By understanding and harnessing the power of environmental design, we can create spaces that naturally support our goals and foster positive habits. This chapter delves into the impact of the environment on behavior, offers practical tips for arranging physical and social environments to support desired habits, and shares case studies of successful environmental design.

The Impact of the Environment on Behavior

The environment we inhabit plays a crucial role in shaping our behaviors and habits. Behavioral scientists have long recognized that our surroundings can either facilitate or hinder our actions. This influence extends to both physical spaces—such as our homes, workplaces, and public areas—and social environments, including the people we interact with and the cultural norms we adhere to.

Physical Environment: The layout and design of spaces can encourage or discourage certain behaviors. For example, a cluttered and disorganized workspace might impede productivity, while a clean, organized desk can enhance focus and efficiency. Similarly, placing healthy snacks at eye level in the kitchen can promote better eating habits, whereas keeping junk food within easy reach can lead to poor dietary choices.

Social Environment: Our social circles have a significant influence on our habits. The behaviors, attitudes, and expectations of those around us can shape our own actions. Positive social influences, such as supportive friends and family, can motivate us to adopt healthy habits. Conversely, negative influences can reinforce undesirable behaviors.

Practical Tips for Arranging Physical Environments to Support Desired Habits

DESIGNING YOUR PHYSICAL Environment to support desired habits involves intentional modifications that make it easier to engage in positive behaviors and harder to succumb to negative ones. Here are practical tips for optimizing your physical spaces:

Declutter and Organize: A clutter-free environment reduces distractions and mental load, making it easier to focus on desired habits. Regularly declutter your living and working spaces, and organize items in a way that promotes efficiency and accessibility.

Create Habit-Friendly Zones: Designate specific areas for particular activities. For example, create a dedicated exercise space in your home with all the necessary equipment readily available. Similarly, set up a quiet reading nook to encourage regular reading habits.

Use Visual Cues: In prominent locations, place visual reminders of your goals and desired habits. Sticky notes, vision boards, and habit trackers can serve as constant motivators. For instance, a sticky note on your bathroom mirror reminding you to floss daily can reinforce this healthy habit.

Simplify Access to Positive Habits: Make it easier to engage in positive behaviors by simplifying access. Keep a water bottle on your desk to remind you to stay hydrated. Place healthy snacks at the front of the fridge and unhealthy ones at the back.

Remove Temptations: Conversely, make it more challenging to engage in undesirable behaviors by removing temptations from your environment. Store junk food in hard-to-reach places, disable notifications on your phone to reduce distractions, and create barriers to time-wasting activities.

Practical Tips for Arranging Social Environments to Support Desired Habits

OPTIMIZING YOUR SOCIAL environment involves fostering relationships and engaging in activities that support your goals. Here are strategies for creating a positive social environment:

Surround Yourself with Supportive People: Seek out friends, family members, and colleagues who share your values and support your goals. Their encouragement and positive influence can help reinforce your desired habits.

Join Communities of Interest: Engage in communities, clubs, or groups that align with your goals. Whether it's a fitness group, a book club, or a professional association, being part of a like-minded community provides accountability and motivation.

Leverage Social Accountability: Share your goals with trusted individuals who can hold you accountable. This could be a workout buddy, a study partner, or a mentor. Regular check-ins and progress updates can keep you on track.

Limit Exposure to Negative Influences: Minimize interactions with individuals or environments that undermine your goals. This might mean distancing yourself from negative influences or avoiding places where you're likely to engage in undesirable behaviors.

Cultivate a Growth Mindset, Culture: Encourage a culture of growth and improvement within your social circles. Share resources, celebrate each other's successes, and provide constructive feedback. A positive and growth-oriented environment fosters collective progress.

Case Studies of Successful Environmental Design

TO ILLUSTRATE THE IMPACT of environmental design, let's explore a few case studies of individuals and organizations that have successfully optimized their environments to support desired habits:

Google's Office Design: Google is renowned for its innovative office designs, which promote productivity and creativity. The company's campuses feature open layouts, abundant natural light, and collaborative spaces. Employees have access to healthy snacks, fitness centers, and relaxation areas. These environmental elements foster a culture of well-being and innovation, enabling employees to thrive.

IKEA's Store Layout: IKEA's store layout is strategically designed to guide customers through a specific path, exposing them to a wide range of products. This design encourages impulse purchases and increases sales. The company's attention to environmental design highlights the power of physical spaces to influence behavior.

Company Culture: Zappos, an online shoe and clothing retailer, places a strong emphasis on company culture. The company fosters a supportive and positive social environment through team-building activities, open communication, and a focus on employee well-being. This culture of support and collaboration has contributed to high employee satisfaction and productivity.

James Clear's Personal Environment: James Clear, the author of Atomic Habits, emphasizes the importance of environmental design in his own life. He organizes his workspace to minimize distractions, keeps healthy snacks visible, and uses habit trackers to monitor his progress. By intentionally designing his environment, Clear has cultivated habits that align with his goals.

Designing your environment for success is a powerful strategy for habit formation and personal growth. By understanding the impact of physical and social environments on behavior and implementing practical tips for arranging these environments, you can create spaces that naturally support your goals. The case studies of successful environmental design demonstrate the profound influence of intentional modifications on fostering positive habits.

Whether it's decluttering your home, joining a supportive community, or leveraging visual cues, the key is to design environments that make it easier to engage in desired behaviors and harder to fall into negative patterns. Through thoughtful environmental design, you can create a foundation for lasting success and personal transformation. Embrace the power of your surroundings, and take proactive steps to shape an environment that nurtures your best self.

Chapter Five

Overcoming Obstacles: Motivation and Willpower

Creating new habits and sustaining them can be a challenging endeavor. Among the most significant barriers are the fluctuating levels of motivation and willpower that everyone experiences. This chapter explores common obstacles to habit formation, provides techniques for boosting motivation and conserving willpower, and introduces the concept of "friction" and how to reduce it to facilitate lasting behavioral change.

Addressing Common Barriers to Habit Formation

One of the primary barriers to habit formation is the lack of consistent motivation. Motivation is often misunderstood as a constant state of enthusiasm, but in reality, it is a fluctuating resource influenced by various factors, including mood, energy levels, and external circumstances. Similarly, willpower is another finite resource that depletes with use, making it difficult to rely on for sustained habit formation.

Inconsistent Motivation: Motivation can be high when we set out to adopt a new habit but tends to wane over time. This decline can be discouraging and lead to abandoning the habit altogether.

Willpower Depletion: Willpower functions like a muscle; it gets fatigued with overuse. As we make decisions and resist temptations throughout the day, our willpower reserves get depleted, leaving us vulnerable to old habits.

Techniques for Boosting Motivation and Preserving Willpower

TO OVERCOME THESE BARRIERS, we need strategies to boost motivation and conserve willpower, ensuring that our habits are sustainable even when motivation is low and determination is running thin.

Boosting Motivation:

CONNECT WITH YOUR 'WHY': Understanding the deeper reason behind your habit can provide a powerful source of motivation. Reflect on why this habit matters to you and how it aligns with your values and long-term goals. Keeping this 'why' in mind can help sustain motivation even during challenging times.

Set SMART Goals: Specific, Measurable, Achievable, Relevant, and Time-bound (SMART) goals provide clarity and direction. Breaking down larger goals into smaller, manageable tasks can make the process less daunting and more achievable.

Visualize Success: Visualization techniques can enhance motivation by helping you imagine the positive outcomes of your new habit. Spend a few minutes each day visualizing yourself successfully performing the habit and enjoying the benefits it brings.

Reward Yourself: Incorporate immediate rewards for sticking to your habit. These rewards can be small treats, breaks, or positive affirmations. Immediate gratification helps reinforce the habit loop, making the routine more appealing.

Conserving Willpower:

AUTOMATE DECISIONS: To reduce decision fatigue, create routines and automate as many decisions as possible. Plan your day ahead, prepare meals in advance, and set specific times for activities to minimize the number of choices you need to make.

Use Implementation Intentions: Formulate specific action plans that link cues to desired behaviors. For example, "If I feel stressed, I will take three deep breaths." These pre-planned responses can help you act on habits without relying on willpower.

Prioritize Self-care: Adequate sleep, nutrition, and exercise are essential for maintaining willpower. When your body and mind are well-rested and nourished, your ability to resist temptations and make healthy choices improves.

Focus on One Habit at a Time: Trying to change multiple habits simultaneously can overwhelm your willpower. Instead, focus on one habit at a time until it becomes automatic before introducing another.

Introducing the Cconceptof "Friction" and How to Reduce It

"FRICTION" REFERS TO the obstacles and resistance that make it harder to perform a desired behavior. By reducing friction, we can make it easier to adopt and maintain new habits. Here are strategies to minimize friction:

Simplify The Process:

STREAMLINE ACTIONS: Break down your habit into the simplest possible steps. The easier and more straightforward the behavior, the less resistance you'll encounter. For example, if your goal is to exercise, start with a 5-minute routine that doesn't require special equipment or a gym visit.

Prepare in Advance: To reduce friction, prepare everything you need ahead of time. Lay out your workout clothes the night before, prep ingredients for healthy meals, or set up your workspace for productivity.

Create Positive Triggers:

DESIGN YOUR ENVIRONMENT: Arrange your environment to support your habits. Place cues in strategic locations to remind you of your goals. For instance, put your running shoes by the door, keep a water bottle on your desk, or set an alarm for reading time.

Remove Negative Triggers: Identify and eliminate cues that prompt undesirable behaviors. This could mean removing junk food from your kitchen, disabling notifications on your phone, or avoiding environments that tempt you to stray from your goals.

Increase Accountability:

SEEK SOCIAL SUPPORT: involve friends, family, or colleagues in your habit formation journey. Share your goals and progress with them, and ask for their support and encouragement. Social accountability can provide an extra layer of motivation and reduce friction.

Use technology: leverage apps and tools designed to track habits and provide reminders. These digital aids can help you stay on course and offer reinforcement when your motivation wanes.

Design Default Choices:

SET DEFAULTS: Create default choices that align with your desired habits. For example, set your default browser homepage to a productivity site, subscribe to healthy meal delivery services, or schedule automatic transfers to your savings account.

Limit Alternatives: To reduce decision fatigue, limit the number of options available. Fewer choices make it easier to stick to your desired habits. For instance, having a limited wardrobe can simplify dressing decisions, and keeping a simple grocery list can streamline healthy eating.

Case Studies for Overcoming Obstacles

CONSIDER THE EXAMPLE of an individual trying to build a habit of daily reading. Initially, they struggle with inconsistent motivation and a lack of willpower to read after a long day at work. They successfully overcame these obstacles by implementing the following strategies:

Connecting with the 'Why': They remind themselves that reading enriches their knowledge and provides relaxation.

Automating Decisions: They set a specific time for reading each evening and create a cozy reading nook with all necessary materials within reach.

Simplifying the Process: They start with just 10 minutes of reading per day, gradually increasing the duration as the habit becomes ingrained.

Creating Positive Triggers: Each morning, they place their current book on their pillow as a reminder to read before bed.

Seeking Social Support: They join a book club, gaining motivation and accountability from fellow members.

Overcoming obstacles like fluctuating motivation and limited willpower is crucial for successful habit formation. By understanding these barriers and employing techniques to boost motivation and conserve willpower, we can create a foundation for lasting change. Additionally, by reducing friction and designing environments that support our goals, we make it easier to adopt and maintain new habits. Embrace these strategies to navigate the challenges of habit formation and transform your behaviors, paving the way for personal growth and success.

Chapter Six

The Role of Identity in Habit Formation

The journey of habit formation is not merely about changing actions; it is about transforming one's identity. Our identity, or the way we perceive ourselves, profoundly shapes our behaviors and habits. Understanding and harnessing the power of identity can lead to lasting change, as habits that align with our self-concept are more likely to stick. This chapter delves into how identity shapes behavior and habits, guides readers on aligning their identity with their goals, and offers exercises for developing a habit-supportive self-image.

How Identity Shapes Behavior and Habits

Identity plays a pivotal role in determining our actions and routines. The beliefs we hold about ourselves influence our decisions and behaviors, often subconsciously guiding our choices. When our habits align with our identity, they become more sustainable and ingrained. Conversely, habits that conflict with our self-concept are harder to maintain.

Identity-Based Habits: behaviors rooted in identity are more enduring because they are part of who we are. For instance, a person who identifies as a "healthy eater" is more likely to choose nutritious foods consistently because this behavior aligns with their self-image.

Cognitive Dissonance: When our actions contradict our identity, we experience cognitive dissonance, a state of psychological discomfort. To reconcile this dissonance, we either change our behavior to align with our identity or modify our identity to justify our actions. Recognizing and leveraging this principle can help us adopt and maintain desired habits.

Beliefs and Self-Efficacy: Our beliefs about our abilities, known as self-efficacy, influence our actions. High self-efficacy leads to greater persistence and resilience in pursuing habits. By cultivating a strong, positive identity, we can boost our self-efficacy and enhance our capacity for habit formation.

Linking Identity with Goals

ALIGNING OUR IDENTITY with our goals involves redefining how we see ourselves and ensuring our self-concept supports our desired behaviors. Here are steps to help readers align their identity with their goals:

Clarify your Desired Identity.

REFLECT ON YOUR GOALS: Identify the habits you want to develop and the goals you aim to achieve. Consider the type of person who consistently engages in these behaviors.

Define Your Desired Identity: Articulate the identity that aligns with your goals. For example, if your goal is to run a marathon, your desired identity might be "I am a dedicated runner."

Adopt Identity-Affirming Beliefs:

CHALLENGE LIMITING Beliefs: Identify and challenge any beliefs that conflict with your desired identity. Replace them with positive affirmations that support your new self-concept. For instance, replace "I'm not a morning person" with "I am someone who enjoys starting the day early."

Affirm Your Identity: Use positive affirmations and self-talk to reinforce your desired identity. Repeatedly affirming "I am a disciplined and focused person" can help internalize this identity.

Act in Alignment with your Identity:

TAKE SMALL STEPS: Start with small, consistent actions that align with your desired identity. Each action, no matter how minor, reinforces your self-concept and builds momentum.

Reflect on Progress: Regularly reflect on your progress and acknowledge the actions you've taken that align with your desired identity. Celebrate these wins to strengthen your self-concept.

Surround yourself with reinforcements.

Seek social support: engage with communities and individuals who embody your desired identity. Their influence and support can reinforce your new self-concept.

Design Your Environment: Create a physical and social environment that supports your desired identity. For example, if you identify as a writer, you should create a dedicated writing space and connect with other writers.

Exercises for Developing a Habit-Supportive Self-Image

TO CULTIVATE A HABIT-supportive self-image, it's essential to engage in exercises that reinforce your desired identity and make it an integral part of who you are. Here are some practical exercises:

Identity Statement Exercise:

WRITE A CLEAR AND CONCISE identity statement that encapsulates your desired self-concept. For example, "I am a confident and healthy individual who prioritizes fitness."

Repeat this statement daily, especially before engaging in related habits. Over time, this affirmation will help solidify your new identity.

Visualization Exercise:

SPEND A FEW MINUTES each day visualizing yourself embodying your desired identity. Imagine how you look, feel, and act like this person. Visualization strengthens neural pathways, making it easier to adopt identity-based habits.

Focus on specific scenarios where you exhibit behaviors aligned with your new identity. For instance, visualize yourself confidently completing a workout or making healthy food choices.

Behavior Journaling:

MAINTAIN A JOURNAL where you document behaviors and actions that align with your desired identity. Reflect on these actions daily and note how they make you feel.

Use this journal to identify patterns, celebrate successes, and address any challenges. Regular journaling helps reinforce your identity through continuous reflection and affirmation.

Identity Role Models:

IDENTIFY ROLE MODELS who embody the identity you aspire to adopt. Study their behaviors, habits, and mindsets. Learn from their experiences and incorporate similar practices into your life.

To stay inspired and motivated, engage with content (books, podcasts, articles) created by or about these role models.

Habit Stacking:

HABIT STACKING IS USED to integrate new habits with existing ones. Identify a current habit and combine it with a new behavior that aligns with your desired identity. For example, if you want to adopt the identity of a reader, stack reading a book for 10 minutes after your morning coffee.

Habit stacking leverages the stability of existing routines to build new, identity-supportive behaviors.

Understanding and leveraging the power of identity is crucial for successful habit formation. Our identity shapes our behaviors and habits, influencing our actions at a subconscious level. By aligning our identity with our goals, adopting identity-affirming beliefs, and taking consistent actions, we can cultivate a self-concept that supports our desired habits.

Exercises such as crafting identity statements, visualization, behavior journaling, learning from role models, and habit stacking provide practical ways to develop a habit-supportive self-image. These practices help us internalize our desired identity, making it an integral part of who we are.

In your habit formation journey, embrace the power of identity. Transform how you see yourself, and let this new self-concept guide your actions and behaviors. By aligning your identity with your goals, you pave the way for lasting change and personal growth.

Chapter Seven

The Power of Tracking and Accountability

Creating and maintaining new habits is a complex process that involves more than just setting goals and taking action. It requires consistent monitoring and accountability to ensure long-term success. Tracking progress and staying accountable are vital components of habit formation, as they provide the necessary feedback and support to keep you on track. This chapter delves into the importance of tracking and accountability, introduces various methods for tracking habits, and suggests ways to build accountability systems through partnerships or groups.

The Importance of Tracking Progress

Tracking progress is an essential part of habit formation because it provides tangible evidence of your efforts and accomplishments. It allows you to see how far you've come and identify areas that need improvement. Here's why tracking progress is crucial:

Measurement Drives Improvement

AS THE MANAGEMENT ADAGE goes, "What gets measured gets managed." Tracking helps you quantify your progress, making it easier to identify trends, set benchmarks, and make necessary adjustments.

Increased Awareness:

TRACKING YOUR HABITS helps you become more aware of your behaviors and patterns. This heightened awareness enables you to make informed decisions about your actions and stay focused on your goals.

Motivation and Encouragement:

SEEING YOUR PROGRESS can be highly motivating. It provides a sense of accomplishment and reinforces your commitment to your goals. Tracking also helps you celebrate small wins, which can boost your morale and keep you engaged.

Accountability:

KEEPING A RECORD OF your habits holds you accountable to yourself. It serves as a reminder of your commitments and encourages consistency. When you see gaps or inconsistencies, you're prompted to take corrective action.

Methods for Tracking Habits

THERE ARE VARIOUS METHODS for tracking habits, each with its own benefits. Here are some effective ways to track your progress:

Journals:

Daily Logs: Maintain a daily log where you record your habits and reflect on your progress. Write down what you did, how you felt, and any challenges you faced. This method helps you stay mindful and provides a detailed record of your journey.

Bullet journals are a versatile tool that combines habit tracking with goal setting, planning, and reflection. You can create customized trackers for different habits and use symbols or colors to indicate completion.

Apps:

HABIT TRACKING APPS: Numerous apps are designed specifically for tracking habits. These apps offer features like reminders, streaks, and progress charts. Popular habit-tracking apps include Habitica, Streaks, and HabitBull.

Fitness and Health Apps: If your habits are related to fitness or health, apps like MyFitnessPal, Strava, or Fitbit can help you monitor your activities, track your progress, and set goals.

Spreadsheets:

Digital Spreadsheets: To track your digital habits, create a spreadsheet. You can use tools like Excel or Google Sheets to design a personalized tracker with columns for dates, habits, and notes. Spreadsheets allow for simple data analysis and visualization.

Visual Trackers:

HABIT TRACKERS: Use a physical habit tracker, such as a calendar or a habit-tracking chart. Each day you complete a habit, mark it off, creating a visual representation of your progress. The act of marking off days can be satisfying and motivating.

Building Accountability Systems

ACCOUNTABILITY SYSTEMS provide external support and motivation, making it easier to stay committed to your habits. Here are ways to build effective accountability systems:

Accountability Partnerships:

FINDING A PARTNER: Choose a friend, family member, or colleague who shares similar goals or is supportive of your efforts. On a regular basis, share your goals and progress with them, and ask that they hold you accountable.

Schedule regular check-ins with your accountability partner. These can be weekly or bi-weekly meetings where you discuss your progress, challenges, and plans for the future.

Accountability Groups:

JOIN A GROUP: LOOK for groups or communities that focus on habit formation or specific goals, such as fitness groups, writing clubs, or professional development circles. Being part of a group provides a sense of camaraderie and shared purpose.

Create Your Own Group: If you can't find an existing group, consider starting one. Invite friends or colleagues who have similar interests and goals. Set up regular meetings, either in person or online, to discuss progress and offer support.

Online Communities:

SOCIAL MEDIA GROUPS: Join social media groups or forums related to your goals. These online communities provide a platform for sharing experiences, seeking advice, and celebrating achievements.

Accountability Apps: Some habit-tracking apps include social features that allow you to connect with others, join challenges, and share your progress. Apps like Habitica turn habit tracking into a game, where you can team up with friends to complete tasks and earn rewards.

Professional Support:

COACHES AND MENTORS: Hiring a coach or mentor can provide personalized guidance and accountability. Coaches help you set realistic goals, develop strategies, and stay on track.

Therapists and counselors: If your habits are related to mental health or behavior change, working with a therapist or counselor can offer additional support and accountability.

Studies of Successful Tracking and Accountability

Fitness Journey:

JOHN'S TRANSFORMATION: John wanted to lose weight and improve his fitness. He started using a fitness app to track his workouts and meals. He also joined a local running club for accountability and support. By consistently tracking his progress and participating in group activities, John stayed motivated and achieved his fitness goals.

Writing Habit:

SARAH'S WRITING ROUTINE: Sarah aspired to write a novel, but she struggled with consistency. She created a bullet journal to track her daily writing sessions and word count. Sarah also joined a writing group that met weekly for writing sprints and feedback sessions. The combination of tracking and group accountability helped Sarah develop a steady writing routine and complete her novel.

Healthy Eating:

LINDA'S DIETARY CHANGES: Linda aimed to adopt healthier eating habits. She used a nutrition app to log her meals and track her nutrient intake. Linda also partnered with a friend who had similar goals, and they shared meal plans and recipes. The app provided data-driven insights, while the partnership offered mutual support, leading to lasting dietary changes.

Tracking progress and staying accountable are essential elements of successful habit formation. By monitoring your habits and seeking external support, you can enhance your commitment, stay motivated, and achieve lasting change. Whether you use journals, apps, spreadsheets, or visual trackers, the key is to find a method that works for you and stick with it. Building accountability systems through partnerships, groups, online communities, or professional support adds another layer of motivation and ensures you stay on track.

Embrace the power of tracking and accountability in your habit formation journey. These tools provide the feedback and support necessary to overcome obstacles, celebrate successes, and maintain consistency. Making tracking and accountability integral parts of your process paves the way for lasting, positive change in your life.

Chapter Eight

Habit Stacking: Building on Existing Routines

In the quest for effective habit formation, the concept of habit stacking offers a powerful strategy for embedding new behaviors into our daily routines. Habit stacking leverages existing routines to create new habits, making the process more seamless and sustainable. This chapter explores the concept of habit stacking, its benefits, and provides a detailed guide for creating habit stacks, along with examples of effective stacks.

Understanding Habit Stacking

Habit stacking is a method introduced by James Clear in his book *Atomic Habits*. The idea is simple: instead of trying to build a new habit from scratch, you attach it to an existing routine. By stacking a new habit onto an existing one, you create a predictable cue that triggers the new behavior. This approach capitalizes on the automatic nature of established routines, making it easier to incorporate new habits into your life.

Benefits of Habit Stacking:

Leverages Existing Routines:

MINIMIZES EFFORT: By linking a new habit to an existing routine, you reduce the mental effort required to remember and implement the new behavior. This reduces the cognitive load and makes the habit formation process more manageable.

Increases Consistency: Existing routines are already ingrained in your daily life, which means you're more likely to perform the new habit consistently when it's attached to something you already do.

Builds Momentum:

SMALL WINS: Habit-stacking allows you to experience small victories more frequently. Completing a habit stack provides a sense of accomplishment, which reinforces your motivation and commitment.

Reinforces Behavior: The satisfaction of completing one habit encourages you to follow through with the next. This positive reinforcement creates a chain reaction that helps solidify the new behavior.

Creates a Routine Chain:

EFFICIENT HABIT FORMATION: Habit stacking enables you to build a series of linked behaviors. Each new habit reinforces the previous one, creating a chain of routines that supports your overall goals.

Consistency and Integration: Over time, the stacked habits become a natural part of your routine. This integration helps ensure that the new behaviors become automatic and sustainable.

Step-By-Step Instructions for Creating Habit Stacks

CREATING EFFECTIVE habit stacks involves a systematic approach. Here's a step-by-step guide to help you design and implement your own habit stacks:

Identify Existing Routines:

List Your Routines: Start by listing the routines and habits you already perform on a regular basis. These can include morning rituals, work routines, or evening activities.

Choose a Stable Routine: Select a routine that is consistently performed and well-established. This will serve as the anchor for your new habit.

Define your New Habit:

BE SPECIFIC: Clearly define the new habit you want to establish. Ensure it is specific, actionable, and realistic. For example, instead of "exercise more," choose "do 10 push-ups."

Align with Goals: Ensure the new habit aligns with your overall goals and fits naturally with the existing routine.

Design Your Habit Stack:

CREATE A SEQUENCE: Determine where, in the existing routine, the new habit will fit. Identify the precise moment when you'll perform the new behavior. For example, if your routine includes brushing your teeth, you might develop the habit of flossing immediately afterward.

Write It Down: Document your habit stack in a visible place, such as a journal or planner. Clearly outline the sequence and ensure it is simple to follow.

Implement and Track:

START SMALL: Begin by implementing the habit stack on a small scale. Focus on consistency rather than perfection.

Monitor Progress: Using a habit tracker or journal, track your progress. When you finish the habit stack, record any challenges or successes.

Adjust and Refine:

EVALUATE EFFECTIVENESS: Periodically review your habit stack to assess its effectiveness. Determine if any adjustments are needed to improve consistency or alignment with your goals.

Make adjustments based on your observations: Refine as necessary. If a particular stack isn't working, consider modifying the timing or sequence to better fit your routine.

Examples of Effective Habit Stacks

HERE ARE SOME PRACTICAL examples of habit stacks that illustrate how to effectively integrate new habits into existing routines:

Morning Routine Stack:

DRINKING A CUP OF COFFEE in the morning is an existing routine.

New Habit: Practicing five minutes of mindfulness meditation.

Stack: After you pour your coffee, take five minutes to sit quietly and meditate. The act of making coffee serves as a cue for your meditation practice.

Evening Routine Stack:

EXISTING ROUTINE: BRUSHING your teeth before bed.

Writing a journal entry is a new habit.

STACK: After brushing your teeth, take a few minutes to write a brief journal entry. The act of brushing your teeth triggers the habit of journaling.

Work Routine Stack:

EXISTING ROUTINE: At the start of the workday, check your email.

New Habit: Reviewing your daily goals.

STACK: After you finish checking your email, take a moment to review and prioritize your daily goals. The email check serves as the cue for goal setting.

Exercise Routine Stack:

EXISTING ROUTINE: Putting on workout clothes in the morning.
 New Habit: doing a short stretching routine.
 Stack: As soon as you put on your workout clothes, immediately perform a series of stretches. The act of changing clothes serves as a cue to stretch.

Meal Prep Stack:

PREPARING DINNER IS an existing routine.
 New Habit: Planning tomorrow's Meals.
 Stack: While cooking dinner, take a few minutes to plan and prep ingredients for the next day's meals. The act of preparing dinner serves as a cue for meal planning.
 Habit stacking is a powerful strategy for integrating new behaviors into your daily routine by leveraging existing habits. By connecting new habits to well-established routines, you can create a seamless and sustainable process for habit formation. Habit stacking has the following benefits: increased consistency, momentum, and the creation of a routine chain that supports your overall goals.

Follow the step-by-step guide to design and implement your own habit stacks, and use the examples provided as inspiration. By systematically integrating new habits into your existing routines, you pave the way for lasting change and personal growth. Embrace the power of habit stacking and watch as small, incremental changes lead to significant, positive transformations in your life.

Chapter Nine

Making Time for New Habits

In the fast-paced rhythm of modern life, finding time to establish and maintain new habits can be challenging. The key to integrating new habits into a busy schedule lies in prioritization, effective scheduling, and creative integration. This chapter offers strategies to carve out time in your packed calendar, underscores the importance of prioritizing and scheduling new habits, and provides actionable tips for seamlessly incorporating them into your daily routine.

Strategies for Finding Time in a Busy Schedule

Conduct a Time Audit.

Track Your Time: Begin by recording how you spend your time over the course of a week. This audit will help you identify time sinks and unproductive periods. Use a time-tracking app or a simple spreadsheet to log your activities.

Analyze Patterns: Look for patterns in your time usage. Identify pockets of time that can be repurposed for new habits, such as breaks, waiting periods, or downtime.

Prioritize Tasks:

IDENTIFY HIGH-IMPACT Activities: Focus on activities that offer the most significant benefits or align with your goals. Prioritize these tasks over less critical activities. For example, if improving fitness is a goal, prioritize exercise over less impactful tasks.

Eliminate or Delegate: Assess tasks that can be eliminated or delegated. By removing non-essential activities or delegating them, you free up time for your new habits.

Optimize your Routine:

COMBINE TASKS: Look for opportunities to combine tasks. For instance, listen to educational podcasts or audiobooks while commuting or exercising. This multitasking approach allows you to integrate new habits without requiring additional time.

Use Idle Moments: Utilize idle moments effectively. Whether it's waiting in line or during a commute, use these times for mini-habits like mindfulness, reading, or planning.

Create Time Blocks:

SET DEDICATED TIME Blocks: Allocate specific time blocks in your schedule for new habits. These blocks should be treated as non-negotiable appointments. This structured approach ensures that you consistently dedicate time to your new behaviors.

Start Small: Begin with small time blocks, such as 10–15 minutes. Gradually increase the duration as the habit becomes established. Short, focused sessions are more manageable and less overwhelming.

Leverage Technology:

USE SCHEDULING APPS: Utilize scheduling apps like Google Calendar or Todoist to plan and set reminders for your new habits. These tools help you stay organized and ensure you don't overlook your commitments.

Set Alerts: To remind you to practice your new habits, set alerts or notifications. These reminders help reinforce the behavior and keep you on track.

The Importance of Prioritizing and Scheduling New Habits

Clarity and Focus:

DEFINE YOUR PRIORITIES: Clearly define your priorities and align your new habits with them. Prioritization helps you focus on what matters most and prevents you from spreading yourself too thin.

Avoid Over commitment: Be realistic about the number of new habits you can introduce simultaneously. Over committing can lead to burnout and decreased effectiveness. Start with one or two habits and gradually build upon them.

Consistency and Routine:

ESTABLISH CONSISTENCY: Scheduling new habits at specific times each day helps create a sense of routine and consistency. Consistent timing reinforces the habit and makes it easier to integrate into your life.

Build Momentum: Regularly scheduled habits build momentum. As you consistently perform the habit, it becomes a natural part of your routine, leading to long-term success.

Accountability:

CREATE ACCOUNTABILITY: Scheduling new habits provides a sense of accountability. By committing to specific times and tracking your progress, you hold yourself accountable and increase the likelihood of follow-through.

Share Your Goals: Share your goals and schedules with a friend, family member, or accountability partner. External accountability can provide additional motivation and support.

Tips for Integrating Habits into Daily Routines

Start with Existing Routines:

ANCHOR NEW HABITS: Attach new habits to existing routines. For example, if you already have a morning routine, add your new habit, such as stretching or journaling, immediately after a part of your established routine.

Habit Stacking: Utilize habit stacking, as discussed in Chapter 8, to seamlessly integrate new habits. By linking new behaviors to well-established routines, you create a natural flow that supports habit formation.

Design Your Environment:

OPTIMIZE YOUR SPACE: Arrange your environment to facilitate the new habit. For instance, if your goal is to read more, place books in visible and accessible locations. A well-organized environment reduces friction and makes it easier to adopt new behaviors.

Remove Distractions: minimize distractions that hinder your ability to focus on your new habits. Create a dedicated space or time for your habits to ensure that you can concentrate and engage fully.

Make it Enjoyable:

INCORPORATE ENJOYMENT: Find ways to make your new habits enjoyable. For example, if you're incorporating exercise, choose activities that you find fun or rewarding. Fun habits are more likely to stick and become routine.

Reward Yourself: Implement a reward system to reinforce positive behavior. After completing your new habit, treat yourself to something you enjoy, such as a favorite snack or leisure activity. Rewards create positive associations with the habit.

Use Reminders and Cues

USE VISUAL CUES TO remind yourself of your new habits. Place sticky notes, set alarms, or use habit-tracking apps to prompt you to perform the behavior. Visual reminders help reinforce the habit and keep it top of mind.

Trigger Cues: Create trigger cues that signal the start of your new habit. For example, if your habit is to practice mindfulness, you can use the act of finishing a meal as a trigger to begin your mindfulness session.

Track and Adjust:

MONITOR PROGRESS: Regularly track your progress and evaluate how well the new habits are integrating into your routine. Use journals, apps, or spreadsheets to record your performance and identify areas for improvement.

Adjust as Needed: Be flexible and willing to change your approach if necessary. If a particular time or method isn't working, experiment with different strategies until you find what best fits your schedule and lifestyle.

Examples of Integrating New Habits

Morning Routine:

EXISTING ROUTINE: Preparing Breakfast.

New Habit: drinking a glass of water.

Integration: Place a glass of water next to your breakfast ingredients. Make it a habit to drink water while preparing or eating breakfast.

Workday Integration:

EXISTING ROUTINE: Start your workday with email checks.

New Habit: Practicing deep breathing exercises.

Integration: After checking your emails, take a moment to do a few deep breathing exercises. Set a reminder on your computer to prompt you after email checks.

Evening Routine:

EXISTING ROUTINE: Brushing your teeth before bed.

New Habit: Reading a Chapter from a Book.

Integration: Place a book next to your toothbrush. After brushing your teeth, immediately pick up the book and read a chapter before turning off the lights.

Exercise Routine:

EXISTING ROUTINE: Watching TV in the evening.

New Habit: doing a 10-minute workout.

Integration: Set up a small exercise area in front of your TV. Use commercial breaks or specific TV show times as cues to perform your workout.

Making time for new habits in a busy schedule requires thoughtful planning, effective prioritization, and creative integration. By conducting a time audit, optimizing your routine, and utilizing technology, you can identify and repurpose time for new habits. Prioritizing and scheduling new behaviors ensures clarity, consistency, and accountability.

Integrating new habits into your daily routines involves anchoring them to existing behaviors, optimizing your environment, and making the process enjoyable. Utilize reminders, cues, and tracking to reinforce the new habits and make necessary adjustments.

Embrace these strategies and tips to successfully integrate new habits into your busy life. With thoughtful planning and consistent effort, you can create meaningful and lasting change, making your new habits a natural and rewarding part of your daily routine.

Chapter Ten

The Art of Starting Small

The journey toward achieving significant goals often begins with the smallest of steps. The art of starting small is a transformative concept that can turn seemingly insurmountable objectives into manageable tasks, making progress more attainable and less daunting. This chapter explores the power of initiating change through small, actionable steps, illustrates how to break down goals into bite-sized components, and highlights the psychological benefits of celebrating small wins.

The Importance of Starting With Small, Manageable Actions

Reducing Overwhelm:

BREAKING DOWN BARRIERS: Large goals can feel overwhelming, causing procrastination or inaction. By starting with small actions, you minimize the initial mental barrier to getting started. Smaller tasks seem less intimidating, making it easier to take the first step.

Building Momentum: Small actions create a sense of accomplishment that builds momentum. Each tiny success adds to your confidence and motivation, making it easier to tackle larger tasks as you progress.

Creating a Sense of Achievability:

REALISTIC GOALS: Smaller actions are inherently more achievable than grandiose plans. By setting realistic, incremental goals, you make progress feel more feasible, reducing the risk of burnout and discouragement.

Incremental Progress: Small steps allow for continuous, incremental progress. Each tiny action contributes to the larger goal, creating a steady trajectory toward success. This incremental approach fosters a sense of progress and accomplishment.

Developing Consistent Habits:

HABIT FORMATION: Starting small helps to form new habits. Research suggests that introducing a new behavior in a manageable way increases the likelihood of successful habit formation. Small, consistent actions gradually integrate into your routine, eventually becoming automatic.

Sustainability: Gradual changes are more sustainable. Small actions are easier to incorporate into daily life, leading to long-term adherence and less risk of regression compared to more drastic changes.

Breaking down goals into tiny steps

Define the Big Goal:

CLARIFY YOUR OBJECTIVE: Clearly articulate your main goal. For example, if your goal is to write a book, define what completing the book entails, such as drafting chapters, editing, and publishing.

Identify Milestones: Break the big goal into major milestones. For writing a book, milestones might include completing the outline, finishing the first draft, and editing.

Decompose Milestones Into Smaller Tasks:

SUBDIVIDE TASKS: Take each milestone and break it down into smaller, actionable tasks. For example, if one milestone is to complete the first draft, divide it into tasks like writing each chapter or section.

Create Micro-Tasks: Further decompose tasks into micro-tasks. For writing a chapter, micro-tasks could include researching, drafting the introduction, writing specific sections, and revising.

Set Actionable Steps:

CREATE DAILY OR WEEKLY Goals: Assign specific, actionable steps to daily or weekly schedules. For example, aim to write 500 words a day or complete one chapter every two weeks.

Use a Task List: To track these small actions, maintain a task list or planner. Checking off completed tasks provides a visual representation of progress and reinforces motivation.

Implement A Time Management Strategy

ALLOCATE TIME BLOCKS: Set aside dedicated time blocks for each small task. For example, allocate 30 minutes each morning for writing or 15 minutes each day for research.

Prioritize Tasks: Prioritize tasks based on their importance and deadlines. Tackle high-priority tasks first to ensure that critical components of your goal are addressed promptly.

Psychological Benefits of Achieving Small Wins

Boosting Self-Esteem and Confidence:

POSITIVE REINFORCEMENT: Each small win acts as positive reinforcement, boosting self-esteem and confidence. Success, even in minor tasks, provides a sense of accomplishment and validation, which fuels further effort.

Overcoming Doubts: Achieving small milestones helps overcome self-doubt. As you complete tiny steps, you gain confidence in your ability to achieve the larger goal, reducing anxiety and fostering a positive mindset.

Enhancing Motivation:

SMALL WINS PROVIDE immediate feedback, which is motivating. The sense of accomplishment from completing a task or reaching a milestone reinforces your commitment and enthusiasm.

Creating a Reward System: Celebrating small wins creates a reward system that enhances motivation. Recognize and celebrate each achievement, whether through self-reward or acknowledgment from others.

Building Resilience:

MANAGING SETBACKS: Small wins help you manage setbacks and build resilience. As you encounter challenges, the momentum from previous successes provides the strength to persevere and adjust your approach.

Maintaining Focus: Achieving small milestones keeps you focused on your long-term goal. The progress made through small actions serves as a reminder of your ability to succeed, maintaining your commitment and drive.

Fostering a Growth Mindset:

EMBRACING CONTINUOUS Improvement: Small wins encourage a growth mindset. Each achievement reflects progress and learning, reinforcing the belief that abilities and outcomes can be developed through effort and perseverance.

Encouraging Experimentation: The art of starting small promotes experimentation and learning. As you achieve small wins, you become more open to trying new approaches and refining your strategies.

Examples of Implementing the Art of Starting Small

Fitness Goal:

BIG GOAL: Run a marathon.

Small Steps: Start with short runs, gradually increasing the distance. Begin with 10-minute runs, then extend to 20, 30, and eventually longer runs as your stamina builds.

Celebrate Wins: Acknowledge each milestone, such as completing a 5K or reaching a personal best in distance. Reward yourself with a new workout accessory or a relaxing activity.

Financial Goal:

BIG GOAL: Save $10,000 for a vacation.

Small Steps: Set up a budget, track expenses, and automate small savings deposits. Start saving $50 per month, then increase it as you get used to it.

Celebrate Wins: Celebrate each savings milestone, such as reaching $1,000, with a small treat or outing. To stay motivated, recognize your progress.

Learning a New Skill:

BIG GOAL: Learn a new language.

Small Steps: Start with daily vocabulary practice, then progress to simple sentences and conversations. Use language learning apps, attend language classes, and practice with native speakers.

Celebrate Wins: Celebrate each new milestone, such as completing a lesson or holding a basic conversation, by rewarding yourself with a cultural experience related to the language.

Writing a Book:

BIG GOAL: Complete a book manuscript.

Small Steps: Break down the writing process into chapters, then further into sections or scenes. Set daily or weekly word count goals and focus on one section at a time.

Celebrate Wins: Acknowledge each completed chapter or section with a small reward, such as a favorite treat or a relaxing activity.

The art of starting small is a powerful approach to achieving significant goals by focusing on manageable actions, breaking down tasks, and celebrating incremental progress. By beginning with small, achievable steps, you reduce overwhelm, build momentum, and develop sustainable habits. The psychological benefits of small wins, including boosted confidence, enhanced motivation, and resilience, further reinforce the effectiveness of this approach.

Embracing the art of starting small transforms ambitious goals into achievable realities. Through careful planning, incremental progress, and consistent effort, you can turn your aspirations into accomplishments and experience the profound impact of small actions on your journey to success.

Chapter Eleven

Adapting and Adjusting: Staying Flexible

In the journey of habit formation, flexibility is an often overlooked but crucial component. As you work towards establishing new habits and achieving goals, the ability to adapt and adjust in response to life's unpredictable nature can differentiate between success and stagnation. This chapter delves into the importance of maintaining a flexible approach to habit formation, offers strategies for adjusting habits amidst life changes and setbacks, and provides practical tips for sustaining habits during challenging times.

The Importance of Flexibility in Habit Formation

Navigating Life's Uncertainties:

Unpredictable Events: Life is inherently unpredictable, with unexpected events and changes often disrupting our routines. Flexibility in habit formation allows us to navigate these uncertainties without derailing our progress.

Adaptation and Resilience: A flexible approach helps us build resilience by adapting habits to fit new circumstances rather than abandoning them altogether. This adaptability ensures that habits remain relevant and achievable despite changing conditions.

Maintaining Motivation and Engagement:

AVOIDING RIGIDITY IN habit formation can lead to frustration and burnout when things don't go as planned. By staying flexible, you can adjust your approach to stay engaged and motivated, even when facing obstacles.

Reinvigorating Habits: Flexibility enables habit renewal and rejuvenation. Adjusting your habits in response to your evolving needs and interests keeps them fresh and meaningful, enhancing your commitment and enjoyment.

Promoting Long-Term Success:

FLEXIBILITY ENCOURAGES sustainable change by allowing habits to evolve in response to ongoing life experiences. This adaptability helps you maintain long-term success, as habits are continuously refined to fit your current situation.

Continuous Improvement: A flexible mindset encourages ongoing assessment and improvement of habits. Regularly reviewing and adjusting your habits ensures that they remain effective and aligned with your goals, fostering continuous personal growth.

Adjusting Habits in Response to Life's Changes and Setbacks

Recognizing the Need for Change:

ASSESSING IMPACT: When faced with life changes or setbacks, assess how these circumstances impact your habits and goals. For instance, a new job with longer hours might affect your exercise routine or personal time.

Identifying Barriers: Identify the specific barriers or challenges that arise from these changes. Understanding the nature of the obstacles enables you to address them effectively and make informed adjustments.

Reassessing and Changing Habits

Revisiting Goals: Revisit your goals and assess whether they need to be adjusted in light of the changes. For example, if your goal was to exercise for an hour daily but your schedule is now more constrained, consider modifying the goal to 30 minutes of exercise or incorporating shorter, more intense workouts.

Adjusting Routines: Change your routines to suit new circumstances. This might involve shifting the timing of your habits, changing the frequency, or adapting the methods you use. Flexibility in routine adjustments ensures that your habits remain feasible and effective.

Developing Alternative Strategies:

EXPLORING NEW APPROACHES: Develop alternative strategies that accommodate your changing situation. If regular gym visits are no longer feasible, explore home workouts or outdoor activities as substitutes.

Implementing Short-Term Solutions: Use short-term solutions to address immediate challenges while working towards long-term adjustments. For example, if traveling disrupts your meal planning, use meal delivery services or easy-to-prepare recipes as a temporary fix.

Maintaining Consistency During Setbacks:

EMBRACING FLEXIBILITY: Understand that setbacks are a natural part of the process. Instead of abandoning your habits, embrace flexibility by adapting them. For instance, if you miss a workout due to illness, adjust your schedule to accommodate a recovery period and resume your routine when possible.

Staying Focused: While adjusting specific habits, stay focused on the overall goal. Remember that the ultimate objective remains the same, even if the path to achieving it needs to be modified.

Strategies for Maintaining Habits During Challenging Times

SETTING REALISTIC EXPECTATIONS:

Adjusting Standards: During challenging times, adjust your expectations to align with your current capacity. For example, if you're managing a stressful situation, aim for smaller, more manageable habit goals, such as 10 minutes of meditation instead of an hour.

Being Compassionate: practice self-compassion and acknowledge that it's okay to modify your habits in response to difficulties. Recognize that progress, even if slower, is still progress.

Creating a Flexible Routine:

ESTABLISHING PRIORITIES: Prioritize essential habits and create a flexible routine that accommodates your changing needs. Designate specific times for key habits, but allow for adjustments based on your availability and circumstances.

Incorporating Adaptable Elements: Include adaptable elements in your routine, such as adjustable time slots or variable activities. This flexibility ensures that you can maintain habits even when faced with fluctuations in your schedule.

Utilizing Support Systems:

Seeking Accountability: To maintain responsibilities, engage support systems, such as friends, family, or habit-tracking groups. Support systems can provide encouragement, motivation, and practical advice during challenging times.

Share your progress and challenges with others to gain perspective and support. Discussing your experiences with a supportive network can help you stay on track and find creative solutions to obstacles.

Implementing Mindfulness and Self-Care:

PRACTICING MINDFULNESS: To manage stress and maintain focus, incorporate mindfulness techniques. Mindfulness can help you stay grounded and make thoughtful adjustments to your habits without becoming overwhelmed.

Prioritizing Self-Care: To support your overall well-being, prioritize self-trouble oneself. Engaging in self-care activities helps you stay balanced and resilient, making it easier to adapt your habits in response to challenges.

Reassessing and Celebrating Progress

REGULAR REVIEWS: Conduct regular reviews of your habits and progress. Assess how well your adjustments are working, and make further modifications as needed to stay aligned with your goals.

Celebrating Milestones: Celebrate accomplishments and achievements, even if they are smaller than initially planned. Recognizing and celebrating progress reinforces your commitment and provides motivation to continue.

The art of adapting and adjusting is vital for successful habit formation and long-term goal achievement. Embracing a flexible approach allows you to navigate life's uncertainties, maintain motivation, and achieve sustainable change. By recognizing the need for adjustments, reevaluating habits, and implementing strategies for maintaining habits during challenging times, you can continue progressing and reaching your goals despite obstacles.

Flexibility in habit formation is not about abandoning your objectives but rather about adapting your approach to fit your evolving circumstances. Through thoughtful adjustments, realistic expectations, and a supportive mindset, you can overcome setbacks and continue moving forward on your path to success. The ability to stay flexible and resilient transforms challenges into opportunities for growth, ensuring that your habits remain effective and meaningful in every phase of your journey.

Chapter Twelve

Celebrating Progress and Reinforcing Habits

In the journey of personal development and habit formation, celebrating progress and reinforcing habits are crucial components that often go underappreciated. The act of recognizing milestones, rewarding oneself in healthy ways, and using positive reinforcement not only enhances motivation but also solidifies the foundation of new habits. This chapter delves into the significance of celebrating achievements, offers creative ideas for rewarding oneself, and explores how positive reinforcement can fortify habit formation.

Celebrating Milestones and Progress

Enhancing Motivation:

Recognizing Achievements: Celebrating milestones provides tangible evidence of progress, which is crucial for maintaining motivation. By acknowledging the effort and success at various stages, you reinforce the value of persistence and hard work.

Boosting Self-Efficacy: Celebrations act as a reminder of your capabilities and achievements, enhancing self-efficacy—the belief in your ability to achieve your goals. This increased self-confidence fuels continued effort and commitment to habit formation.

Reinforcing Positive Behavior:

AFFIRMING SUCCESS: Recognizing and celebrating progress confirms the effectiveness of your efforts and strategies. This affirmation strengthens the connection between your actions and desired outcomes, making it more likely that you will continue those behaviors.

Creating Positive Associations: Celebrations help create positive associations with the habits you are trying to build. When progress is associated with positive feelings, you are more likely to stay committed to the habit.

Fostering a Growth Mindset:

EMBRACING PROGRESS: Celebrating milestones fosters a growth mindset by emphasizing the value of continuous improvement. It helps you view setbacks as opportunities for learning rather than failures, encouraging resilience and adaptability.

Acknowledging Effort: Celebrations emphasize the importance of effort and persistence over mere outcomes. This focus on effort promotes a positive attitude towards the habit-building process and reinforces the idea that progress, however incremental, is valuable.

Deas for Rewarding Oneself in Healthy, Supportive Ways

Setting Meaningful Rewards:

FOR EXAMPLE, IF YOU'VE achieved a fitness milestone, treat yourself to a new workout outfit or a relaxing spa day. To maximize its effectiveness, the reward should resonate with you personally.

Experiential Rewards: Opt for experiential rewards that create lasting memories, such as a weekend getaway, a cooking class, or a concert. Experiences often provide more lasting satisfaction than material possessions and can contribute to overall well-being.

Healthy and Sustainable Rewards:

NON-FOOD REWARDS: While food-related rewards can be tempting, consider alternatives that support your overall health and well-being. For example, indulge in a new book, a hobby, or a self-care activity that promotes relaxation and enjoyment.

Incremental Rewards: Implement a system of incremental rewards for small milestones. This approach ensures that you stay motivated throughout the process, rather than waiting for a significant achievement to celebrate.

Social and Community-Based Rewards:

SHARING ACHIEVEMENTS: Share your successes with friends, family, or a support group. Celebrating together not only reinforces your progress but also fosters a sense of community and support.

This communal approach can enhance the joy of your achievements and strengthen social connections.

Self-Care and Relaxation:

PAMPERING YOURSELF: Treat yourself to self-care activities that help you relax and recharge. This might include a massage, a quiet day of reflection, or a favorite relaxation ritual. Self-care rewards contribute to overall well-being and help you maintain balance.

Positive Reinforcement Strengthens habit formation.

Building Consistency:

WHEN YOU RECEIVE POSITIVE feedback or rewards for completing a habit, it reinforces the behavior, making it more likely to become ingrained in your routine.

Creating Positive Feedback Loops: Positive reinforcement creates feedback loops where desired behaviors are continually reinforced, leading to greater consistency and stability in your habits.

Enhancing Habit Formation:

THE MORE FREQUENTLY you receive rewards, the more ingrained the habit becomes in your brain's wiring.

Encouraging Repetition: The anticipation of rewards encourages repeated practice of the habit, which is essential for its establishment. The more you engage in the behavior and receive positive reinforcement, the more likely it is to become a lasting habit.

Motivating Continued Effort:

THIS ONGOING MOTIVATION is crucial for overcoming challenges and maintaining progress towards your goals.

Fostering Enjoyment: When you receive positive reinforcement, it enhances the enjoyment and satisfaction derived from the habit. This increased enjoyment makes the habit more appealing and reinforces your commitment to maintaining it.

Addressing Setbacks:

OVERCOMING CHALLENGES: Positive reinforcement can help you overcome setbacks by providing motivation to get back on track. Celebrating small successes and rewarding yourself for resilience in the face of challenges reinforces your ability to persevere and adapt.

Celebrating progress and reinforcing habits are integral to the process of personal growth and habit formation. Recognizing milestones, rewarding yourself in healthy and supportive ways, and leveraging positive reinforcement can help you increase motivation, solidify new habits, and foster long-term success.

The act of celebrating achievements, no matter how small, reinforces the value of your efforts and creates positive associations with your habits. Choosing meaningful, healthy rewards and incorporating positive reinforcement strategies not only strengthens habit formation but also ensures that your journey is both enjoyable and sustainable.

By embracing the power of celebration and positive reinforcement, you unlock the potential for continued growth and achievement. By recognizing your progress, rewarding yourself, and reinforcing your habits, you pave the way for lasting success and fulfillment in every aspect of your life.

Chapter Thirteen

Stories of Transformation: Real-Life Examples

The journey of mastering habits through small actions is a testament to the transformative power of incremental changes. Real-life stories of individuals who have successfully navigated this path offer powerful lessons in perseverance, strategy, and the profound impact of seemingly minor adjustments. This chapter will delve into inspiring stories of transformation, analyze the common elements and strategies behind these success stories, and extract valuable lessons and takeaways that can guide others on their own journey of personal growth.

Inspiring Stories of Transformation

James Clear: From Overcoming Adversity to Becoming a Bestselling Author

Background: James Clear, author of Atomic Habits, is a prime example of how small actions can lead to extraordinary results. Clear's journey began after a severe injury in a baseball accident during high school, which left him with a long road to recovery.

Transformation: Clear used his recovery period as an opportunity to cultivate habits that would aid his physical and mental healing. He focused on incremental improvements in his health and productivity, which laid the groundwork for his future success as a writer and speaker.

Lessons: Clear's story highlights the power of consistency and the importance of focusing on small, manageable changes. His approach to habit formation—breaking down complex goals into simple, actionable steps—demonstrates the effectiveness of habit stacking and gradual progress.

Marie Kondo: Revolutionizing the Art of Tidying Up

Background: Marie Kondo, the author of The Life-Changing Magic of Tidying Up, started her career as a professional organizer in Japan. Her method, known as the KonMari Method, focuses on decluttering by category rather than location.

Transformation: Kondo's approach involved small, daily actions that gradually led to significant changes in her clients' lives. By encouraging people to keep only items that "spark joy," she helped them transform their living spaces and mental well-being.

Lessons: Kondo's success underscores the importance of aligning habits with personal values and creating a system that simplifies the process of maintaining new behaviors. Her method demonstrates how small, purposeful actions can lead to profound and lasting changes in one's environment and mindset.

David Goggins: From overweight and depressed to Navy SEAL and Ultra-Endurance Athlete

Background: David Goggins, a retired Navy SEAL and ultra-endurance athlete, overcame a troubled childhood and significant health issues to achieve extraordinary physical and mental feats.

Transformation: Goggins implemented a regimen of rigorous physical training and mental discipline, starting with small, consistent actions that gradually built his strength and resilience. His commitment to incremental progress helped him achieve remarkable endurance and mental fortitude.

Lessons: Goggins' story exemplifies the power of perseverance and the importance of embracing discomfort and challenges. His approach to habit formation—setting high standards, pushing through adversity, and maintaining a focus on small, incremental improvements—offers valuable insights into achieving personal and professional goals.

J.K. Rowling: From Struggling Single Mother to Global Literary Phenomenon

Background: J.K. Rowling, the author of the Harry Potter series, faced numerous challenges before achieving success. As a single mother struggling with poverty, she wrote her first manuscript in cafes while her child slept.

Transformation: Rowling's persistence and dedication to her writing, despite the difficulties she faced, exemplify the power of small, consistent efforts. Her ability to maintain a daily writing routine and overcome rejection played a crucial role in her eventual success.

Lessons: Rowling's journey highlights the importance of resilience and the value of small, daily efforts in achieving long-term success. Her story demonstrates that consistent, focused work, even in the face of adversity, can lead to extraordinary outcomes.

Common Elements and Strategies in Success Stories

Consistency and Persistence:

INCREMENTAL PROGRESS: Each of these individuals demonstrated that success is built upon a foundation of consistent, incremental actions. By focusing on small, manageable steps, they were able to make steady progress toward their goals.

Overcoming Setbacks: The ability to persist through challenges and setbacks was a common theme. These individuals maintained their focus and continued their efforts despite obstacles, illustrating the importance of resilience in achieving long-term success.

Alignment with Personal Values:

PURPOSE-DRIVEN ACTIONS: Many of these success stories involve aligning habits with personal values and goals. Whether through decluttering, physical training, or creative writing, each individual's approach was deeply connected to their core beliefs and motivations.

Authenticity: These individuals' success also stemmed from their authenticity and commitment to their chosen paths. They pursued goals that were meaningful to them, which helped sustain their motivation and dedication.

Strategic Habit Formation:

OWN GOALS: Successful individuals often break goals into smaller, actionable steps. This approach made their goals more manageable and allowed them to focus on gradual improvements.

Systems: To form effective habits, one must create structures and routines that support their goals. Through organizing their environment, setting specific routines, or using positive reinforcement, these individuals developed strategies that facilitated their success.

Positive Reinforcement:

MILESTONES: Recognizing and celebrating small achievements was a common element in their stories. This positive reinforcement helped sustain motivation and reinforced their commitment to their habits.

Progress: Each individual found ways to reward themselves for progress, whether through personal treats, shared celebrations, or public recognition. These rewards reinforced their habits and provided ongoing motivation.

NS and Takeaways

The Power of Small Actions:

INCREMENTAL IMPROVEMENT: The success stories demonstrate that small actions, consistently applied, can lead to significant transformations. Focusing on manageable steps and gradual progress is a key strategy for achieving long-term success.

Sustaining Motivation: Celebrating milestones and recognizing progress are essential for maintaining motivation and reinforcing habits. Positive reinforcement and rewards help sustain commitment and drive continued effort.

Resilience and Adaptability

OVERCOMING CHALLENGES: The ability to persevere through setbacks and challenges is crucial for achieving success. Each of these individuals faced obstacles but remained resilient and adaptable, demonstrating the importance of persistence in habit formation.

Embracing Change: Adapting habits in response to changing circumstances and new insights is a key factor in long-term success. Flexibility and a willingness to adjust strategies as needed contribute to sustained progress and achievement.

Alignment with Values:

PURPOSEFUL ACTIONS: Aligning habits with personal values and goals enhances motivation and commitment. Pursuing meaningful goals and staying true to personal beliefs provide a strong foundation for habit formation and success.

Authentic Pursuit: Authenticity and dedication to one's chosen path are essential for achieving extraordinary outcomes. Each individual's success was driven by their genuine passion and commitment to their goals.

Creating Effective Systems:

STRATEGIC PLANNING: Developing systems and routines that support habit formation is critical for success. Breaking down goals, creating supportive environments, and implementing positive reinforcement are effective strategies for achieving long-term results.

Building Resilience: Cultivating resilience and adaptability helps overcome challenges and maintain progress. By staying focused on incremental improvements and celebrating achievements, individuals can navigate setbacks and continue their journey toward success.

The stories of transformation shared in this chapter illustrate the profound impact of small actions and consistent efforts in mastering habits. By examining these real-life examples, we gain valuable insights into the strategies and principles that underpin successful habit formation. From consistency and resilience to alignment with personal values and strategic planning, these lessons offer a roadmap for achieving personal and professional goals. Embracing the power of small actions, celebrating progress, and reinforcing habits pave the way for lasting transformation and fulfillment in every aspect of life.

Chapter Fourteen

Beyond Personal Habits: Influencing Others

The journey to mastering personal habits is often a transformative experience, reshaping not only our own lives but also potentially influencing those around us. When we become adept at forming and maintaining habits, we unlock the ability to inspire and positively impact others. This chapter explores how the principles of behavior mastery can be leveraged to influence family members, friends, and colleagues and examines the broader ripple effect that personal habit changes can have on communities and organizations.

Applying Behavior Mastery Principles to Influence Others

LEAD BY EXAMPLE.

Leading by example is one of the most effective ways to influence others. Demonstrating the positive changes and successes you've achieved through habit mastery can serve as a powerful motivator for those around you. When people see the tangible benefits of your new habits, they are more likely to be inspired to adopt similar behaviors.

Key Strategies:

Show Consistency: Consistently practicing your habits will naturally draw attention. For instance, if you've adopted a new exercise routine and are visibly more energetic and healthier, others may be inspired to follow suit.

Share Your Journey: Openly discussing your experiences and the positive impacts of your habits can provide valuable insights and encouragement to others. This transparency fosters a supportive environment where others feel more comfortable trying new habits themselves.

Understanding and Addressing Barriers

TO EFFECTIVELY INFLUENCE others, it is crucial to understand the barriers they face and address them thoughtfully. Just as you faced challenges in forming your habits, others may encounter their own obstacles.

Key Strategies:

Empathize with Challenges: Engage in conversations to understand the specific difficulties others face in adopting new habits. Use your own experience to offer practical solutions or adjustments that could help them overcome these hurdles.

Provide Support and Resources: Offer resources, such as articles, tools, or workshops, that address common barriers. Additionally, consider providing emotional support and encouragement to help them navigate their own habit-forming journey.

Foster a Positive Environment

Creating an environment conducive to habit formation can have a significant influence on others. When the environment supports and reinforces desired behaviors, it becomes easier for people to adopt and maintain new habits.

Key Strategies:

Create Habit-Friendly Spaces: Design spaces that encourage positive behaviors. For example, if promoting a healthier lifestyle, ensure that healthy snacks and exercise equipment are easily accessible.

Encourage Group Participation: form or join groups focused on shared goals, such as fitness clubs or study groups. A group's collective energy and support can boost motivation and accountability.

Tips for Helping Family Members, Friends, and Colleagues Adopt New Habits

Communicate Effectively

EFFECTIVE COMMUNICATION is essential when helping others adopt new habits. Tailor your approach to the individual's preferences and needs to ensure that your message resonates.

Key Strategies:

Use positive reinforcement: Focus on the benefits and positive aspects of the new habit rather than emphasizing shortcomings or criticisms. Positive reinforcement can be more motivating and less intimidating.

Provide clear and actionable steps. Break down the habit adoption process into clear, manageable steps. Offering a structured plan can make the process less overwhelming and more achievable.

Encourage gradual change.

Encouraging gradual change rather than immediate, sweeping modifications can lead to more sustainable habit adoption. Small, incremental adjustments are often easier to integrate into daily life and can lead to lasting results.

Key Strategies:

Start Small: Suggest starting with small, manageable changes that can be gradually built upon. For example, if you're encouraging a healthier diet, start by adding one serving of vegetables to each meal rather than overhauling the entire diet at once.

Celebrate Small Wins: Recognize and celebrate small achievements along the way. Acknowledging progress helps build confidence and motivation, reinforcing the desire to continue making positive changes.

Offer Personalized Support.

Each individual's journey to adopting new habits is unique. Personalized support tailored to their specific needs and preferences can significantly enhance their chances of success.

Key Strategies:

Set Individual Goals: Collaborate with the person to create personalized, achievable goals that align with their interests and motivations. Customizing goals ensures that they are relevant and meaningful, increasing the likelihood of commitment.

Provide Ongoing Feedback: Offer regular feedback and encouragement. Personalized feedback helps individuals stay on track and adjust their approach as needed.

The ripple effect of personal habit change on communities and organizations

The Impact on Family and Friends

WHEN AN INDIVIDUAL successfully adopts new habits, the benefits often extend to their family and friends. Positive changes in one person's life can create a ripple effect, encouraging others to make similar improvements.

Key Insights:

INFLUENCE ON FAMILY Dynamics: Improved habits, such as healthier eating or increased physical activity, can enhance family members' overall well-being. The shared experience of adopting new habits can strengthen family bonds and promote a healthier lifestyle for everyone.

Encouragement for Friends: Friends who observe positive changes may be inspired to make their own improvements. Sharing success stories and providing support can encourage friends to embark on their own habit-forming journeys.

Influence on Workplace Culture

PERSONAL HABIT CHANGES can also influence workplace culture. When employees adopt positive habits, such as improved time management or effective communication, it can enhance overall productivity and morale.

Key Insights:

FOSTERING A SUPPORTIVE Work Environment: Encouraging habits that promote well-being and efficiency can create a more supportive and collaborative work environment. Initiatives such as wellness programs or team-building activities can reinforce positive behaviors and strengthen workplace relationships.

Driving Organizational Change: Individuals who model positive habits have the potential to inspire organizational change. Their behaviors can serve as a catalyst for broader initiatives, such as improving workplace practices or implementing new policies that benefit the entire organization.

Community and Social Impact

ON A LARGER SCALE, personal habit changes can contribute to community and societal well-being. When individuals adopt habits that promote health, sustainability, or social responsibility, the impact can extend beyond their immediate circles.

Key Insights:

PROMOTING PUBLIC HEALTH: Individuals who embrace healthy habits, such as regular exercise or nutritious eating, can contribute to broader public health initiatives. Their example can encourage others to prioritize their well-being, leading to a healthier community overall.

Supporting Social Causes: Adopting social responsibility-related habits, such as volunteering or reducing waste, can influence others to engage in similar activities. The collective impact of these efforts can drive positive change within communities and contribute to societal progress.

Influencing others with the principles of behavior mastery entails leading by example, understanding and addressing barriers, and creating supportive environments. By applying these strategies, we can help family members, friends, and colleagues adopt new habits and contribute to positive change. The ripple effect of personal habit changes extends to families, workplaces, and communities, demonstrating the profound impact that individual actions can have on broader societal transformations. Embracing the power of small actions and fostering a culture of support and encouragement can drive meaningful and lasting change, benefiting individuals and society as a whole.

Chapter Fifteen

Sustaining Long-Term Change

Embarking on the journey of habit formation is a remarkable achievement, but the true challenge lies in maintaining these habits over time. The ability to sustain long-term change requires a strategic approach, ongoing motivation, and a commitment to continuous improvement. This chapter delves into effective strategies for maintaining habits, the importance of periodic review and adjustment, and insights into staying motivated for enduring success.

Strategies for Maintaining Habits over the Long Term

Establish a Routine and Rituals.

Creating a consistent routine and incorporating rituals can significantly enhance the sustainability of new habits. Routines provide structure and predictability, making it easier to integrate habits into daily life.

Key Strategies:

INTEGRATE HABITS INTO Daily Routines: Embed your habits into existing routines to ensure they become a natural part of your day. For example, if you're trying to develop a habit of reading, set aside a specific time each day, such as before bed, to read a few pages.

Create Rituals: Develop small rituals that signal the start of your habit. Rituals can act as mental cues, reinforcing the habit's importance and making it more enjoyable. For instance, if your goal is to exercise, your ritual might include laying out your workout clothes the night before.

Implement Habit Stacking

HABIT STACKING INVOLVES linking a new habit to an existing one, leveraging the established behavior to anchor the new habit. This technique makes it easier to adopt new habits by piggybacking on behaviors that are already ingrained.

Key Strategies:

IDENTIFY EXISTING HABITS: Determine which habits are firmly established in your routine and use them as anchors for new behaviors. For example, if you already have a morning coffee ritual, you could stack a new habit of stretching or meditating onto this routine.

Create Simple, Actionable Steps: Ensure that the new habit is simple and easy to perform. This reduces the cognitive load and increases the likelihood of consistent practice. For example, if your existing habit is brushing your teeth, you might stack a habit of flossing right afterward.

Set Long-Term Goals and Milestones

LONG-TERM GOALS PROVIDE direction and purpose, while milestones offer a way to track progress and celebrate achievements. Both are essential for maintaining motivation and ensuring that habits continue to align with overarching objectives.

Key Strategies:

DEFINE CLEAR LONG-TERM Goals: Establish specific, measurable, achievable, relevant, and time-bound (SMART) goals that provide a sense of purpose and direction. For example, if your goal is to improve physical fitness, set a long-term goal of participating in a marathon within a year.

Track Progress with Milestones: Break down long-term goals into smaller, manageable milestones. Celebrate these milestones to maintain motivation and acknowledge progress. For instance, if your long-term goal is to lose weight, set intermediate milestones for monthly weight loss targets and reward yourself for reaching them.

The Importance of Periodic Review and Adjustment

Evaluate Progress Regularly

REGULAR EVALUATION of your progress is crucial for sustaining long-term change. It allows you to assess the effectiveness of your habits, identify areas for improvement, and make necessary adjustments.

Key Strategies:

Schedule Regular Check-Ins: Set aside time periodically, such as weekly or monthly, to review your progress. Use this time to assess how well your habits are aligning with your goals and whether any adjustments are needed.

Reflect on Successes and Challenges: Reflect on what has worked well and where you've faced challenges. This reflection provides valuable insights into areas that may need modification or improvement.

Adjust Habits and Strategies as Needed

FLEXIBILITY AND ADAPTABILITY are essential for sustaining long-term change. As circumstances evolve and new challenges arise, it is important to adjust your habits and strategies accordingly.

Key Strategies:

Be Open to Change: Recognize that what worked initially may need to be adjusted over time. Be willing to modify your approach based on your evolving needs and circumstances. For example, if your initial exercise routine becomes monotonous, consider trying new activities to maintain interest and motivation.

Experiment with New Strategies: Don't be afraid to experiment with different strategies and techniques. This experimentation can help you discover more effective ways to maintain your habits and achieve your goals.

Staying Motivated and Committed to Continuous Improvement

Cultivate a Growth Mindset

ADOPTING A GROWTH MINDSET is essential for maintaining motivation and commitment. A growth mindset embraces challenges, values effort, and sees failures as opportunities for learning and improvement.

Key Strategies:

Embrace Challenges: View challenges as opportunities for growth rather than obstacles. When faced with difficulties, focus on the lessons learned and the progress made rather than on setbacks.

Celebrate Effort and Improvement: Recognize and celebrate your efforts and improvements, regardless of the outcome. This positive reinforcement reinforces the value of persistence and encourages continued commitment.

Stay Connected to Your "Why"

UNDERSTANDING AND STAYING connected to your underlying motivations and reasons for adopting new habits is crucial for long-term success. A strong sense of purpose helps sustain motivation and commitment.

Key Strategies:

Articulate Your Purpose: Clearly define why each habit is important to you and how it aligns with your broader goals and values. Writing down your reasons and reviewing them regularly can help reinforce your commitment.

Visualize Success: Regularly visualize the positive outcomes of your habits and the impact they will have on your life. Visualization helps maintain motivation and provides a tangible reminder of your goals.

Build a Support System

HAVING A SUPPORT SYSTEM can greatly enhance your ability to maintain habits and stay motivated. Surrounding yourself with people who encourage and support your efforts can provide accountability and inspiration.

Key Strategies:

Seek Out Accountability Partners: Identify individuals who share similar goals or interests and establish accountability partnerships. Regular check-ins and mutual support can help keep you on track and motivated.

Engage with Supportive Communities: Participate in communities or groups related to your habits or goals. Engaging with others who are also working towards similar objectives can provide additional motivation and encouragement.

Prioritize Self-Care

MAINTAINING GOOD HABITS requires a balanced approach to self-care. Taking care of your physical, emotional, and mental well-being ensures that you have the energy and resilience needed to stay committed.

Key Strategies:

Practice Regular Self-Care: Incorporate self-care activities into your routine, such as exercise, relaxation, and hobbies. Prioritizing self-care helps reduce stress and maintain overall well-being.

Monitor Your Well-Being: Pay attention to your physical and emotional health. If you notice signs of burnout or fatigue, make adjustments to your habits or seek support as needed.

Sustaining long-term change requires a thoughtful and strategic approach. By establishing consistent routines, setting long-term goals, and implementing periodic review and adjustment, you can maintain habits over time. Staying motivated and committed involves cultivating a growth mindset, staying connected to your purpose, and building a supportive network. Prioritizing self-care ensures that you remain resilient and energized on your journey. Embracing these strategies will help you achieve lasting success and continue to evolve towards continuous improvement, making your habits a powerful force for positive change in your life.

Chapter Sixteen

The Journey to Behavior Mastery

As we draw the final curtain on our exploration of behavior mastery, it's essential to reflect on the journey we've undertaken and the profound insights we've uncovered. The path to mastering behavior and transforming habits is not just a quest for personal development; it's a transformative journey that redefines our approach to life, goals, and achievements. This concluding chapter summarizes the key takeaways from our journey, encourages readers to embrace the ongoing quest for behavior mastery, and offers motivational insights to propel them forward into their own habit transformation.

Summarizing Key Points and Takeaways

The Science of Small Actions

The foundation of behavior mastery lies in understanding the science of small actions is the foundation of behavior mastery. We've explored how small, manageable changes can lead to significant improvements over time. By focusing on incremental adjustments, we harness the power of the compound effect, where tiny behaviors accumulate into remarkable results. Recognizing that profound change begins with small steps empowers us to break down our goals into actionable tasks, making them more achievable and sustainable.

Identifying and Leveraging Keystone Habits

IDENTIFYING KEYSTONE habits—the cornerstone behaviors that drive other positive changes—has been crucial to our understanding of behavior mastery. By focusing on these pivotal habits, we can create a ripple effect that influences various aspects of our lives. These keystone habits serve as anchors, facilitating the development of other desired behaviors and contributing to overall growth and success.

The Habit Loop: Cue, Routine, and Reward

THE HABIT LOOP FRAMEWORK has illuminated the intricate relationship between cues, routines, and rewards. By dissecting this loop, we've learned how to modify each element to foster new habits or reshape existing ones. Understanding this framework equips us with the tools to engineer positive behavior changes, enhance consistency, and overcome obstacles that may arise.

Designing Environments for Success

OUR EXPLORATION OF environmental design highlighted the profound impact that our surroundings have on our behavior. By strategically arranging our physical and social environments, we can create an atmosphere conducive to success. Practical tips for environmental design empower us to reduce friction, remove temptations, and reinforce our commitment to positive habits.

Overcoming Obstacles: Motivation and Willpower

WE DELVED INTO THE challenges of maintaining motivation and willpower, identifying techniques to bolster these essential traits. Understanding the concept of friction and strategies to minimize it helps us navigate barriers and sustain our habits. By implementing practical methods to boost motivation and conserve willpower, we position ourselves for long-term success.

The Role of Identity in Habit Formation

IDENTITY PLAYS A PIVOTAL role in shaping our behavior. Aligning our identity with our goals helps us foster a habit-supportive self-image and reinforces our commitment to change. Exercises for developing a habit-supportive self-image allow us to cultivate a mindset that embraces growth and transformation.

The Ability to Track and Hold People Accountable

TRACKING PROGRESS AND staying accountable are integral to behavior mastery. Various methods for tracking habits, including journals and apps, provide valuable insights into our journey. Building accountability systems through partnerships or groups enhances our commitment and ensures continued progress.

Habit Stacking and Making Time for New Habits

WE EXPLORED THE EFFECTIVENESS of habit stacking—linking new habits to existing ones—and strategies for finding time in a busy schedule. By integrating new habits into our daily routines and breaking down goals into manageable steps, we maximize our ability to adopt and sustain positive behaviors.

The Art of Starting Small

STARTING WITH SMALL, manageable actions is a key principle of behavior mastery. By breaking down goals into tiny steps and celebrating small wins, we build momentum and foster a positive mindset. This approach reinforces our commitment and encourages continuous progress.

Adapting and Adjusting: Staying Flexible

FLEXIBILITY AND ADAPTABILITY are essential for sustaining long-term change. Adjusting our habits in response to life changes and setbacks ensures that we remain resilient and committed. Strategies for maintaining habits during challenging times help us navigate obstacles and stay on course.

Celebrating Progress and Reinforcing Habits

CELEBRATING MILESTONES and reinforcing progress are vital components of behavior mastery. By rewarding ourselves in healthy and supportive ways, we strengthen our habits and maintain motivation. Positive reinforcement helps solidify our commitment and fosters a sense of accomplishment.

Stories of Transformation: Real-Life Examples

REAL-LIFE STORIES OF individuals who mastered their habits through small actions provide inspiration and valuable lessons. Analyzing common elements and strategies in these success stories sheds light on effective approaches and encourages us to apply these principles to our own lives.

Beyond Personal Habits: Influencing Others

APPLYING BEHAVIOR MASTERY principles to influence others positively extends the impact of our personal transformation. By helping family members, friends, and colleagues adopt new habits, we create a ripple effect that fosters collective growth and improvement.

Sustaining Long-Term Change

MAINTAINING LONG-TERM habits necessitates ongoing strategies, periodic review, and a commitment to continuous improvement. By cultivating a growth mindset, staying connected to our purpose, and building a supportive network, we ensure enduring success and progress.

Embracing the Journey of Behavior Mastery

THE JOURNEY TO BEHAVIOR mastery is a continuous and evolving process. It's a path of self-discovery, growth, and transformation that extends beyond achieving specific goals. Embracing this journey involves recognizing that behavior mastery is not a destination but an ongoing pursuit of excellence and improvement.

Embrace the Process

APPROACH BEHAVIOR MASTERY with an open mind and a willingness to learn. Recognize that setbacks and challenges are integral to the journey and provide opportunities for growth. Embrace the process of self-discovery and personal development, knowing that each step forward contributes to your overall success.

Stay Committed to Continuous Improvement.

COMMITMENT TO CONTINUOUS improvement ensures that you remain on the path of behavior mastery. Regularly assess your progress, set new goals, and seek opportunities for growth. By adopting a lifelong learning and development mindset, you stay motivated and engaged in your journey.

Celebrate your achievements.

Celebrate your achievements and milestones, no matter how small. Recognizing and acknowledging your progress reinforces your commitment and provides motivation to continue. Celebrate both the journey and the destination, and use your accomplishments as fuel for further success.

Final Motivational Insights and Call to Action

AS YOU EMBARK ON YOUR journey to behavior mastery, remember that the power to transform your habits and achieve your goals lies within you. The principles and strategies explored in this book provide a roadmap for creating lasting change and fostering personal growth.

Believe in Your Potential

BELIEVE IN YOUR POTENTIAL to achieve greatness and make meaningful changes in your life. Embrace the journey with confidence and a positive mindset, knowing that each step forward brings you closer to your goals.

Take Action Today

DON'T WAIT FOR THE perfect moment to start your habit transformation journey. Take action today, no matter how small. Begin by implementing one of the strategies or techniques discussed in this book and build momentum from there.

Seek Support and Guidance

SEEK SUPPORT AND GUIDANCE from mentors, coaches, or supportive communities. Surround yourself with individuals who inspire and encourage you on your journey. Collaboration and accountability enhance your ability to sustain long-term change.

Keep Moving Forward

THE PATH TO BEHAVIOR mastery is a continuous journey of growth and improvement. Keep moving forward, even when faced with challenges. Stay committed to your goals, embrace the process, and celebrate your progress along the way.

In conclusion, the journey to behavior mastery is a profound and transformative experience. By embracing the principles and strategies outlined in this book, you can achieve lasting change, cultivate positive habits, and unlock your full potential. Take the first step today, and embark on a journey that will redefine your life and lead you to remarkable success.

Don't miss out!

Visit the website below and you can sign up to receive emails whenever Jack Hill publishes a new book. There's no charge and no obligation.

https://books2read.com/r/B-A-NEFZB-RASZD

BOOKS 2 READ

Connecting independent readers to independent writers.